REVISE AQA GCSE (9–1)

English Langua

PRACTICE PAPERS Plus+

Series Consultant: Harry Smith

Author: Julie Hughes

Reviewer: Esther Menon

These Practice Papers are designed to complement your revision and to help prepare you for the exams. They do not include all the content and skills needed for the complete course and have been written to help you practise what you have learned. They may not be representative of a real exam paper. Remember that the official AQA specification and associated assessment guidance materials are the only authoritative source of information and should always be referred to for definitive guidance.

For further information, visit the AQA website.

Contents

About this book

The practice papers in this book are designed to help you prepare for your AQA English Language examinations.

In the margin of each paper you will find:

- links to relevant pages in the Pearson Revise AQA English Language (9–1) Revision Guide
- hints to get you started on tricky questions, or to help you avoid common pitfalls
- help or reminders about important phrases or key terms
- advice on how to get top marks in the higher-level questions.

If you want to tackle a paper under exam conditions, you could cover up the hints in the margin.

There are also answers to all the questions at the back of the book, together with information about how marks are allocated. Many of these are sample model student answers, especially for the longer writing questions. This means that there are many answers which could be given, so you could answer the question differently and still gain full marks. The model answer could still give you new ideas to help you to improve an answer.

About the papers

Look at the time guidance at the top of each paper if you wish to practise under exam conditions.

Remember that in the exam:

- You should use a black ink or ball-point pen.
- You should read every question carefully and answer all the questions in the space provided.
- Try to check your answers if you have time at the end.

Good luck!

Paper 1: Explorations in creative reading and writing

Time allowed: 1 hour 45 minutes

There are 40 marks for Section A and 40 marks for Section B

The source that follows is:

Source A: 20th Century prose-fiction
Frenchman's Creek by Daphne du Maurier
It is an extract from a novel first published in 1941, but set in an earlier time.

In this extract, Dona, the main character in the story, is walking along a narrow, sheltered river – a creek – near her home in Cornwall when she comes across the hiding place of French pirates.

She followed the track that she had found in the morning, but this time plunging down deep into the woods without hesitation. The birds were astir again, after their noonday silence, and the silent butterflies danced and fluttered, while drowsy bumble bees hummed in the warm air, winging their way to the topmost branches of the trees. Yes, there once again was the glimmer of water that had surprised her. The trees were thinning, she was coming to the bank – and there, suddenly before her for the first time, was the creek, still and soundless, shrouded by the trees, hidden from the eyes of men. She stared at it in wonder, for she had had no knowledge of its existence, this stealthy branch of the parent river creeping into her own property, so sheltered, so concealed by the woods themselves. The tide was ebbing, the water oozing away from the mud flats, and here, where she stood, was the head of the creek itself, for the stream ended in a trickle, and the trickle in a spring. The creek twisted round a belt of trees, and she began to walk along the bank, happy, fascinated, forgetting her mission, for this discovery was a pleasure quite unexpected, this creek was a source of enchantment, a new escape, better than Navron[1] itself, a place to drowse and sleep, a lotus-land. There was a heron[2], standing in the shallows, solemn and grey, his head sunk in his hooded shoulders, and beyond him a little oyster-catcher[3] pattered in the mud, and then, weird and lovely, a curlew[4] called and, rising from the bank, flew away from her down the creek. Something, not herself, disturbed the birds, for the heron rose slowly, flapping his slow wings, and followed the curlew, and Dona paused a moment, for she too had heard a sound, a sound of tapping, of hammering.

She went on, coming to the corner where the creek turned, and then she paused, withdrawing instinctively to the cover of the trees, for there before her, where the creek suddenly widened, forming a pool, lay a ship at anchor – so close that she could have tossed a biscuit to the decks. She recognized it at once. This was the ship she had seen the night before, the painted ship on the horizon, red and golden in the setting sun. There were two men slung over the side, chipping at the paint, this was the sound of hammering she had heard. It must be deep water where the ship lay, a perfect anchorage, for on either side the mud banks rose steeply and the tide ran away, frothing and bubbling, while the creek itself twisted again and turned, running towards the parent river out of sight. A few yards from where she stood was a little quay. There was tackle there, and blocks, and ropes; they must be making repairs. A boat was tied alongside, but no one was in it.

But for the two men chipping at the side of the ship all was still, the drowsy stillness of a summer afternoon. No one would know, thought Dona, no one could tell, unless they had walked as she had done, down from Navron House, that a ship lay at anchor in this pool, shrouded as it was by the trees, and hidden from the open river.

Another man crossed the deck and leant over the bulwark[5], gazing down at his fellows. A little smiling man, like a monkey, and he carried a lute in his hands. He swung himself up on the bulwark, and sat cross-legged, and began to play the strings. The two men looked up at him, and laughed, as he strummed a careless, lilting air, and then he began to sing, softly at first, then a little louder, and Dona, straining to catch the words, realized with a sudden wave of understanding, and her heart thumping, that the man was singing in French.

Then she knew, then she understood – her hands went clammy, her mouth felt dry and parched, and she felt, for the first time in her life, a funny strange spasm of fear.

This was the Frenchman's hiding-place – that was his ship.

[1]Navron – the name of Dona's house
[2]heron – a large bird found near water
[3]oyster-catcher – a wading bird found near water
[4]curlew – a wading bird found near water
[5]bulwark – the high sides of a ship that prevent people falling overboard

First spend about **15 minutes reading** the source and all five questions you have to answer (in Section A and Section B).

After the reading time, spend about **45 minutes on Section A** – including planning and checking time – and about **5 minutes on Question 1.**

Unlocking the question

Read the question carefully: you are being asked for **four** pieces of information.

Revision Guide
Pages 13–14

Hint

You can use short quotations or paraphrase the source in your answer. Using short quotations will help you to avoid changing the meaning of the text.

Watch out!

Only look at the lines of the source given in the question. You could draw a box around them to remind yourself.

Hint

You only need to **list** the points you find. You don't need to explain or analyse them.

SECTION A – Reading
Answer ALL questions in this section.
You are advised to spend about 45 minutes on this section.

1 Read again the first part of the source from **lines 1 to 4**.
List **four** things from this part of the source about the woods.

(4 marks)

1 ....

....

2 ....

....

3 ....

....

4 ....

....

2 Look in detail at this extract from **lines 8 to 16** of the source:

> The tide was ebbing, the water oozing away from the mud flats, and here, where she stood, was the head of the creek itself, for the stream ended in a trickle, and the trickle in a spring. The creek twisted round a belt of trees, and she began to walk along the bank, happy, fascinated, forgetting her mission, for this discovery was a pleasure quite unexpected, this creek was a source of enchantment, a new escape, better than Navron itself, a place to drowse and sleep, a lotus-land. There was a heron, standing in the shallows, solemn and grey, his head sunk in his hooded shoulders, and beyond him a little oyster-catcher pattered in the mud, and then, weird and lovely, a curlew called and, rising from the bank, flew away from her down the creek. Something, not herself, disturbed the birds, for the heron rose slowly, flapping his slow wings, and followed the curlew, and Dona paused a moment, for she too had heard a sound, a sound of tapping, of hammering.

How does the writer use language here to describe the creek?
You could include the writer's choice of:

- words and phrases
- language features and techniques
- sentence forms.

(8 marks)

....

....

....

....

....

....

....

....

....

....

....

....

....

....

....

....

....

....

....

....

....

....

Time

Spend about **10 minutes** on this question.

Unlocking the question

Read the question carefully and underline **key words** before you start your answer. Use the bullet points in the question as a guide. You don't have to cover all of the bullet points – focus on the ones that are most relevant to the extract.

Hint

Use **explanatory words and phrases** to make your answer clear and to show you are analysing – not just identifying – the language in the source. For example:
This highlights...
This suggests...
This emphasises...
The effect of...

Watch out!

When you write about sentences, don't just label them as single-clause (simple), multi-clause (compound and complex) or minor. Make sure you comment on **why** they have been used and the **effects** they create.
For example, this writer uses several long, multi-clause sentences to build up a detailed picture of the setting.

Revision Guide
pages 31–32

Hint

Use **short, embedded quotations** to help you to focus on, and analyse, the effect of the individual words and phrases. Make sure that any quotations you use are **relevant** to the question.

Revision Guide page 37

Watch out!

When you write about sentence types, you don't need to quote full sentences. Just make it clear which sentence you are writing about – for example, 'A long sentence is then used to show...' You could also use line references – for example, '...the long sentence beginning in line 9...'

Hint

Think about **connotations** – the ideas created by individual words and phrases. Here, for example, the noun 'mission' has connotations of an important journey or goal.

Revision Guide page 20

LEARN IT!

Make sure you are familiar with the correct terminology for a wide range of **word classes** and **language devices**. For example, for this question you would need the following terms: adjectives, verbs, nouns, list.

Revision Guide pages 19 and 27

3 You now need to think about the **whole** of the source.

This text is taken from an early chapter of a novel.

How has the writer structured the text to interest you as a reader?

You could write about:
- what the writer focuses your attention on at the beginning
- how and why the writer changes this focus as the source develops
- any other structural features that interest you.

(8 marks)

Time

Spend about **10 minutes** on this question.

Unlocking the question

Remember to consider **the whole of the source** when writing about structure. Think about the overall sequence of the extract and the effect of the order in which information is revealed to the reader.

Hint

You could use the bullet points in the question to help you structure your response. But remember that you can include your own ideas too.

Hint

Always read the **contextual information** that is given at the start of the source. This will help you to understand where the extract fits into the overall plot.

Watch out!

Keep the **question focus** in mind. Make sure that all of your points focus on the **effects** of the structural features you have identified.

Hint

Use a range of **explanatory phrases** to make your points clear. For example:
The extract starts...
The attention shifts...
The writer builds up...
The perspective changes...
The pace slows...
The focus is shifted...

LEARN IT!

In this type of question, make sure you consider a full range of **structural techniques**, including: pauses in the action; withheld information; changes in narrative perspective, setting or focus; and foreshadowing.

Revision Guide page 29

Watch out!

Back up **all** of your points with **evidence**. Embedded quotations are most effective, but keep them short and focused. When you are writing about structure, it is often useful to refer to the source using the line numbers.

Revision Guide page 37

4 Focus this part of your answer on the second part of the source from **line 17 to the end**.

A student, having read this section of the text, said: 'The writer makes the scene with the ship seem exciting and slightly dangerous. It is as if you are there with Dona, seeing it with her eyes.'

To what extent do you agree?

In your response, you could:

- write about your own impressions of the scene on the ship
- evaluate how the writer has created these impressions
- support your opinions with references to the text.

(20 marks)

....

....

....

....

....

....

....

....

....

....

....

....

....

....

....

....

....

....

....

....

....

....

....

....

....

....

....

Time

Spend about **20 minutes** on this question – **5 minutes planning**, and **15 minutes writing**.

Unlocking the question

Read the question carefully to make sure you understand the focus. Here, the focus is the scene with the ship – you should consider whether you agree that the ship is exciting and dangerous, as well as giving your own impressions.

Unlocking the question

Good answers will cover all three of the bullet points in the question. If you do this, you will be: giving **your own impressions**; considering the **effectiveness** of the writer's language and structural choices; using **evidence** from the source to support each point you make.

Revision Guide
pages 35–37

Hint

This is a **high mark question**. Make sure that you have considered the whole of the extract given in the question, and give yourself enough time to answer.

Hint

Plan your answer before you start writing. Support your planning by annotating the extract with your ideas. Here, for example, you could underline any words or phrases that make the ship seem exciting or dangerous.

Revision Guide page 36

Hint

Remember to support your evaluation with short, embedded quotations.

Revision Guide page 37

LEARN IT!

Make sure you are familiar with a wide range of **language features** – including narrative voice, dialogue, vocabulary, imagery and language devices – and **structural techniques**, such as repetition and shifts in focus.

Revision Guide pages 20–23 and 29

Aim higher

Consider alternative interpretations of the text. Here, for example, the phrase 'the drowsy stillness of a summer afternoon' might seem both threatening and peaceful.

Hint

If you are asked about characters, consider the way they are presented and think about how a reader might react. Here, for example, how might a reader feel about the man described as 'like a monkey'?

Watch out!

Consider the **writer's methods**. You don't need to identify and name every technique that is used – but you do need to show an understanding that the writer has made deliberate **choices** that create particular **effects** for the reader.

SECTION B: Writing

You are advised to spend about 45 minutes on this section.

Write in full sentences. You are reminded of the need to plan your answer.

You should leave enough time to check your work at the end.

5 A magazine has asked for contributions for their creative writing page.

Either: Write a description of a journey as suggested by this picture:

Or: Write a story about finding something frightening.

(24 marks for content and organisation
16 marks for technical accuracy)
(40 marks)

....

....

....

....

....

....

....

....

....

....

....

....

....

Time

Spend about **45 minutes** on Section B – for example, **5 minutes planning, 35 minutes writing, 5 minutes checking** your work.

Unlocking the question

You will be given a **choice of two writing tasks** but you only need to **answer one**. You might have a choice between one description and one narrative task, two description tasks, or two narrative tasks.

Hint

Make a plan before you start writing. If you choose the narrative (story) option, use a simple three-part story structure with a clear **beginning, middle and end**. Think about how your **characters** might develop or be changed by the **events**. Include ideas for a strong ending which will be satisfying for the reader.

Revision Guide page 65

Aim higher

You could consider a four-part structure: **exposition** (beginning), **complication** (introduction of problem), **crisis** (high point), **resolution** (ending). Keep your focus tight – remember that you only have about 35 minutes to complete the story.

Revision Guide page 66

Watch out!

If you choose to answer a description task, make sure you stay focused on **description** rather than narrative.

Hint

Use a wide **variety of sentence lengths and types** to give your writing an engaging pace.

Revision Guide pages 87–89

Watch out!

Avoid over-using **figurative language**. Similes, metaphors and personification – when used with care and for effect – can add atmosphere and create strong pictures in the reader's mind.

Revision Guide pages 21 and 84

Aim higher

Dashes can be used in pairs to add information mid-sentence ('All four children – including the baby – were invited.') or on their own at the end of a sentence, to suggest a pause before an afterthought ('Even the baby was invited – although I can't imagine why.').

Revision Guide page 94

LEARN IT!

Make sure you know the difference between **homophones** (words that sound the same) such as affect/effect, who's/whose and past/passed.

Revision Guide pages 96–97

Watch out!

Don't use too much **dialogue**: focus on describing settings, characters and action in prose. If you do use dialogue, make sure you punctuate it correctly.

Revision Guide page 93

Hint

Choose your **verbs** carefully to show, not tell. For example, instead of 'We all stopped talking as the teacher came into the room looking really angry', you could write 'Silence fell as the teacher marched into the room, folded her arms and glared at us over the top of her glasses'. Here, 'marched' and 'glared' suggest anger without actually saying it.

Revision Guide page 80

Aim higher

An **ellipsis** can be used to add **dramatic tension** at the end of a paragraph ('The room was empty…') – but be careful not to overuse this technique.

Revision Guide page 94

Watch out!

Stick to a consistent **narrative voice** throughout. If you are writing a first person narrative, don't switch to the third person halfway through.

Revision Guide pages 24 and 55

Watch out!

Check you use the **correct tense** throughout. Unless you deliberately change tense by using a flashback, it is probably best to stick to the past tense ('I walk**ed** alone along the shore…').

Hint

Make your sentences more interesting by starting them in different ways. For example, with: a **pronoun** (I, we); an article (the, a); a **preposition** (above, behind); an **'ing' word** (running, hurrying); an **adjective** (slow, quiet); an **adverb** (happily, quickly); a **conjunction** (if, although).

Revision Guide page 88

LEARN IT!

Remember the difference between **its** and **it's**. **It's** is an abbreviation of 'it is', while **its** means something belonging to **it**.

Revision Guide page 96

Aim higher

Use **advanced punctuation** correctly. For example, **semi-colons** can be used instead of a conjunction to link two connected ideas: 'There was no way I was going into the house alone; I was simply too scared.'

Revision Guide page 94

Hint

Engage the reader by using the **senses** to help make your writing more vivid.

Revision Guide page 54

Aim higher

Try to use a **wide range of ambitious vocabulary** – but make sure the words you use fit the context. Build up a bank of exciting synonyms for common verbs like 'walk'.

Revision Guide pages 79–80

Watch out!

Pay attention to content, organisation and technical accuracy – spelling, punctuation and grammar! Your writing for Section B will be marked against all these points. Check your work when you've finished writing.

Revision Guide pages 96-99

Paper 2: Writers' viewpoints and perspectives

Time allowed: 1 hour 45 minutes

There are 40 marks for Section A and 40 marks for Section B

The sources that follow are:

Source A: 21st Century non-fiction

'Giving to charity is selfish – and that's fine' by David Shariatmadari

An extract from a newspaper article about the emotions involved in donating money, published in 2015.

Source B: 19th Century literary non-fiction

'How to Give'

An extract from an advice text published in 1897.

Please turn the page over to see the sources

Source A – 21st Century non-fiction

David Shariatmadari writes about giving money to charity in this extract from an article published in *The Guardian* in 2015.

Giving to charity is selfish – and that's fine

The Guardian, 7 April 2015

As I recently found out, donating money is as much about making ourselves feel good as it is helping others. But it's something that we should embrace.

Last year, moved by a particularly upsetting news story, I decided to make a big donation to charity. Christmas was approaching, and I thought: what if I cut back on presents, and deploy a bit of belt-tightening[1] elsewhere – surely I can manage to find £300 to help a group of people whose lives are falling apart?

It was the largest amount I'd ever given in one go. I don't know if that's impressive or embarrassing – research reported in today's Times suggests that the British public regards £278 as a generous donation – but it's hardly big-time philanthropy[2]. I'm lucky, of course, to be in the position where I can even consider parting with that much money on a whim. But it was still a significant chunk out of my monthly budget.

My charitable habits are modest. I give a small amount to two organisations each month, and almost never make one-off donations. I have never been the type to raise money via feats of physical prowess. I once abseiled down a castle wall as part of a school charity event, but since I'd neglected to find any sponsors at all, no one was any better off for my vertigo.

One reason, I think, is that I feel a bit uncomfortable giving money away. That's convenient, I hear you say. But it's true: I suspect my motives. I reckon that I'm only really doing it to feel good about myself, and that makes me uneasy. But if the price of my purity is that good causes miss out, maybe I should just get over it?

As it happened, my £300 donation was an interesting study in the psychology of giving. I posted a link to the charity on Facebook, telling my friends what I was doing (I didn't specify the amount), and suggesting they did the same. Sacrifice some Christmas presents for a gift that might really make a difference. I was hoping for a multiplier effect. I even tweeted it. Maybe someone huge would RT[3] me and a cascade of giving would ensue. I was proud of myself. I thought of the people I was helping and imagined them in my mind's eye receiving clean water, bedding, shelter. I felt a warm glow.

This warm glow is a very real, physiological[4] phenomenon. In one study, researchers used functional magnetic resonance imaging[5] to look at the effect of donation on the brain. They found increased activity in the ventral striatum[6] during acts of voluntary giving. This is a region associated with reward, one of the areas that bursts into life under the influence of addictive stimulants like cocaine. Charity can get you high.

Well, almost. A month later I was confronted with the flimsiness of my commitment. I hadn't realised it, but when I made the first donation, I had clicked a box that meant it would recur. When I checked my bank statement in January, I was horrified to see that another £300 had flown out of my account and landed in the charity's coffers[7]. I gulped. My first thought was: can I get it back?

Of course I couldn't. The loss of that money would be a serious inconvenience to me. But there was no way I could pretend I was worse off than the people I had wanted to help before Christmas. I was stuck with an act of generosity I hadn't intended, and it felt very strange.

My initial donation had, despite what I thought, been motivated by that warm glow. If it were pure altruism[8], I would have been pleased the extra money had found its way to those in need. Instead, I felt tricked. Well, for a moment anyway, until I realised it would be morally indefensible to act like I was the one who was hard done by.

It was instructive to be exposed in this way, if only to myself. I'm a human being, and the good feeling I get from being generous isn't something I can rise above. Better to acknowledge that giving to charity is selfish, and keep on giving, all the same.

[1] *belt-tightening – spending less money*
[2] *philanthropy – donating money or services to good causes*
[3] *RT – re-tweet*
[4] *physiological – about how the body functions*
[5] *functional magnetic resonance imaging – a way of measuring activity in the brain*
[6] *ventral striatum – the part of the brain that controls decision-making*
[7] *coffers – strong-boxes for holding valuable items*
[8] *pure altruism – unselfish concern for others, kindness*

Source B – 19th Century literary non-fiction

This is an extract from an advice text published in *The Girl's Own Paper* in 1897. *The Girl's Own Paper* was a Victorian magazine aimed at girls and young women. Advice texts were common in Victorian newspapers and magazines, and would have covered a variety of lifestyle topics.

HOW TO GIVE

A friend lately observed that there was no duty more plainly inculcated[1] in the Bible than that of helping the deserving poor, but that there is no more difficult task than to find them.

An immense amount of harm is done by injudicious[2] and ill-considered giving. We cannot bear to see the poor crossing-sweeper boy on a cold and wet day with bare feet and threadbare clothes, or the miserable woman begging, with a still more miserable baby crying for food in her arms, and with a generous impulse we bestow a coin without a thought as to whether or not we are really benefiting the one or the other. In nine cases out of ten such gifts are misplaced. The boy's money is all taken home in fear and trembling to drunken parents, who have no intention of buying him better clothes or sufficient food, and the woman keeps the child (not her own) cruelly ill-fed and ill-clothed in order to excite compassion and get money for her also to waste in drink.

An experienced worker in London has lately stated that in the course of a wide experience he has scarcely ever found a deserving street-beggar, the babies and little children with them are usually hired, and really deserving people do not beg in the street.

It is true that the world would be a dull place indeed without those dear creatures who are moved by impulse in giving and without using their judgement, but great evils are often increased thereby[3].

There are several qualifications needed for successful almsgiving[4], and one must learn how to give. To be a blessing rather than the reverse, a gift should be accompanied by 'sanctified[5] common cause', and due inquiry should be made as to the truth of the appeal made to us. It should also be, if possible, of sufficient amount to be of real and permanent benefit, not only what will satisfy the need of the moment. It is far better to undertake one case and work for it thoroughly till it is placed on a permanent basis of safety than to give small doles to several cases.

'Not grudging or of necessity' should also be in our minds when we give.

Our giving should also be proportionate to our income; by this I mean that we should, at stated times, set aside a proportion of what we have for charitable purposes. This would always then be available, and we should not trust to the impulses of the moment. Many people set aside a tenth of their income, but this may be an undue proportion for people of small means. Yet, that should be aimed at and bring a blessing with it, often in increased prosperity to the giver. To those unaccustomed to such a rule, it may seem hard at first to set aside one shilling[6] out of every ten, but if begun in early life, one gets to look upon that shilling as not one's own to deal with except for charity. If this were universally practised, what vast sums would be available for good works. Bazaars[7] and sales would be quite unnecessary, and there would be no need of the huge expenditure of stationery and stamps as well as of time to secure funds, and what joy there would be to secretaries of charitable societies and the clergy[8] who now have to fret and worry, write and speak day and night in order to get the funds for carrying on the work entrusted to them.

We must not forget, however, that there are gifts besides those of money.

[1]*inculcated – implanted or taught*
[2]*injudicious – foolish or unwise*
[3]*thereby – as a result of this*
[4]*almsgiving – the practice of giving money to poor people*
[5]*sanctified – legitimate*
[6]*shilling – one-twelfth of a pound in old British currency*
[7]*bazaars – marketplaces*
[8]*clergy – officers of the church, such as vicars*

SECTION A – Reading
Answer ALL questions in this section.
You are advised to spend about 45 minutes on this section.

1 Read again the first part of **Source A** from **lines 1 to 13**.
Choose **four** statements below which are TRUE.

- Shade the **circles** in the boxes of the ones that you think are true.
- Choose a maximum of four statements.
- If you make an error cross out the **whole box**.
- If you change your mind and require a statement that has been crossed out then draw a circle around the box.

(4 marks)

A David Shariatmadari gives a large amount to charity every Christmas. ○

B £300 is a large part of David Shariatmadari's monthly budget. ○

C David Shariatmadari thinks £278 is a very generous donation to charity. ○

D David Shariatmadari gives money to two charities every month. ○

E At school, David Shariatmadari had no problems abseiling down a wall for charity. ○

F Raising money for charity by doing something physical doesn't come naturally to David Shariatmadari. ○

G David Shariatmadari feels uncomfortable giving away his money. ○

H David Shariatmadari has no concerns about the motives behind his charitable giving. ○

Time

Before you answer any questions, spend about **15 minutes reading** the sources and all five questions you have to answer (in Section A and Section B).

After the reading time, spend about **45 minutes on Section A** – including planning and checking time – and about **5 minutes on Question 1.**

Unlocking the question

Make your answers clear. You need to **shade the circles in the boxes** next to the statements you think are true.

Watch out!

This question directs you to a specific section of one of the sources. Look **only** at these lines to find the answers. You could draw a line around them to help you focus on the correct text.

Revision Guide
Pages 13–15

Hint

The order of the statements follows the order of the source – so work through the lines of the source in order, one statement at a time.

Time

Spend about **8 minutes** on this question.

Unlocking the question

This question tests your ability to **synthesise** (summarise), so you need to use information from **both sources** in your answer.

Revision Guide Pages 39–41

Unlocking the question

First, identify the **question focus** (here, it is the effect on people of charitable donations). Next, go through each source in turn and underline **relevant textual details**. Then ask yourself: What can I **infer** from the textual details? What are the **differences** between the sources?

Revision Guide Page 15

Hint

To **synthesise** you need to show a full understanding of both sources by selecting relevant information from each and writing about them together.

Watch out!

Make sure you write your answer in **continuous prose** – full sentences organised into paragraphs. Do not answer in bullet points.

Revision Guide Page 74

2 You need to refer to **Source A** and **Source B** for this question.
Both sources discuss different things to consider when giving to charity.
Use details from **both** sources to write a summary of the differences between the things they mention.

(8 marks)

Hint

To structure your synthesis, start with an overview to sum up your main points. Start a new paragraph for each point you make and cover both sources in each paragraph. Include evidence from both sources to support each point.

Watch out!

You can use quotations as evidence in your answer, but remember that you are **not** being asked to analyse the language.

Revision Guide Page 40

Watch out!

Always make it clear which source you are writing about – either by using the writer's name, or by calling them 'Source A' and 'Source B'.

Aim higher

Strong answers will include **perceptive** comments. This means you need to identify and select the most appropriate evidence and use inference to explain the effect of this evidence.

Set A
Paper 2

Time

Spend about **12 minutes** on this question.

Unlocking the question

Before you start your answer, **underline key words** in the question so that you understand the focus. Here, the focus is on the difficulties of giving to charity.

Hint

This question asks you to **analyse the language**. You should consider word classes, language devices, sentence types and lengths, repetition of words and phrases, and contrasts.

Revision Guide
Pages 19, 27–28, 31–32

LEARN IT!

Practise techniques for working out the meaning of **unfamiliar words and phrases**. Often, the text before and after the unfamiliar word or phrase (the context) can help you to infer the meaning.

Watch out!

Remember to **comment on the effect** of a device, word or phrase. Don't just put a quotation into your own words. Use Point – Evidence – Explain (P–E–E) to structure your points.

3 You now need to refer **only** to **Source B** from **lines 1 to 14**.
How does the writer use language to suggest giving to charity is difficult?

(12 marks)

Watch out!

Don't just list every feature you find. Identify features – such as language techniques and sentence types – that are **relevant** to the question focus, then **explain their connotations and effects**. Do this even if you don't know the name of the technique.

Revision Guide Page 20

Aim higher

You could also look at **relevant** punctuation. Here, for example, brackets are used in Source B to give additional information that emphasises the writer's point of view about beggars.

LEARN IT!

Make sure you are familiar with a wide range of **language devices**, **word classes** and **sentence types**. In Source B, for example, you could comment on: personal anecdote, long (multi-clause) and short sentences, emotive language, adjectives, personal pronouns and expert evidence.

Revision Guide
Pages 12 and 19

Time

Spend about **20 minutes** on this question – about **5 minutes planning**, and **15 minutes writing**.

Unlocking the question

Before you start your answer, **underline key words** in the question so that you understand the focus. Here, the focus is on the different attitudes to giving to charity.

Unlocking the question

Make sure you understand the bullet points in the question: **'attitudes'** means **ideas and perspectives**; **'methods'** means the **language and structural techniques** the writers use.

Hint

The question tells you the writers' attitudes are different. Identify the **key differences in their attitudes** at the beginning of your answer.

Unlocking the question

You need to **compare** the sources. This means finding similarities and differences in the attitudes and methods of the writers.

Revision Guide
Pages 39, 42–48

4 For this question, you need to refer to the **whole of Source A**, together with the **whole of Source B**.

Compare how the writers convey their different attitudes to giving to charity.

In your answer, you could:

- compare their different attitudes
- compare the methods they use to convey their attitudes
- support your response with references to both texts.

(16 marks)

Hint

The texts may be similar or different in various ways: ideas, purpose, perspective (viewpoint), language, structure and effect on the reader.

Unlocking the question

One source will always be a 19th-century text and the other will always be from either the 20th or the 21st century.

Hint

Make sure you **use evidence** to support your ideas and **explain the effect** on the reader.

Revision Guide Pages 42–48

Hint

Start by establishing the meaning and purpose of both texts. Then, identify similarities and differences between them.

Watch out!

You must **give the texts equal weighting** in your answer. If you make a point about one text, make a comparative point about the other.

Revision Guide Page 48

Hint

When you consider the writers' attitudes, think about their **tone** – the overall mood created in the writing. For example, does the tone suggest the writer is angry about the topic, or is the tone more humorous?

Hint

It is often easiest to start a comparative paragraph with a similarity. For example: 'Both these texts…' You can then go on to comment on the differences. If you start by identifying a similarity in the writers' ideas, you might go on to comment on differences in the language or structure they use to convey these ideas.

Watch out!

Remember to make it clear which text you are referring to by using the writer's name or calling them 'Source A' or 'Source B'.

Watch out!

You do not need to use every page provided in the answer booklet. If you are regularly needing more paper, you are probably writing too much! Make sure all of your points contain a comparison between the two texts.

LEARN IT!

Make sure you know a wide range of **comparative words and phrases**. For example:
On the other hand…,
Similarly…,
In contrast…,
Both writers…,
However…,
Likewise…,
In the same way…,
While…

Revision Guide
Pages 41 and 48

Time

Spend about **45 minutes** on Section B – for example, **5 minutes planning**, **35 minutes writing**, **5 minutes checking** your work.

Unlocking the question

Read the question carefully before you start to make sure you fully understand the **audience** (here, broadsheet newspaper readers), the **purpose** (here, to explain your view on the statement) and the **form/ text type** (here, an article).

Revision Guide
Pages 52, 56–58, 61–63

Watch out!

Pay attention to content, organisation and technical accuracy – spelling, punctuation and grammar! Your writing for Section B will be marked against all these points. Save five minutes to check your work when you've finished writing and proofread it for mistakes.

Revision Guide
Pages 96–99

Hint

Make a plan before you start writing. First, establish your **viewpoint** on the topic. Then plan your answer by selecting key points that back up that viewpoint.

Revision Guide
Pages 69–70

SECTION B: Writing

You are advised to spend about 45 minutes on this section.
You are reminded of the need to plan your answer.
You should write in full sentences.
You should leave enough time to check your work at the end.

5 'Taking part in events to raise funds for charity is a waste of time. It doesn't actually help anybody in the end.'

Write an article for a broadsheet newspaper in which you explain your point of view on this statement.

(24 marks for content and organisation
16 marks for technical accuracy)

(40 marks)

....
....
....
....
....
....
....
....
....
....
....
....
....
....
....
....
....
....
....
....
....
....
....
....

Watch out!

Make sure you think about how to **sequence your key points** when planning. Adding detail to your plan is useful, but it's important not to forget about **structure**. Stay focused when planning to make sure you still have plenty of time to write.

Hint

Remember that each point you make will need to be developed with **evidence**, such as facts, expert opinions or personal anecdotes.

Hint

Remember to match the **register** of your writing to the purpose, form and audience. Register is about **how formal** your writing is.

Revision Guide
Pages 77–78

Aim higher

Use colloquial language very occasionally for effect – for example, to stop the tone of your writing becoming too formal. Make sure you choose any examples you include with care – keep your audience and purpose in mind!

LEARN IT!

Learn the spellings of common **homophones** (words that sound the same), such as your/you're, there/their/they're, to/too/two, allowed/aloud, we're/where/wear/were, of/off, past/passed and our/are.

Revision Guide Pages 96–97

Hint

Link your paragraphs together clearly to help your audience follow your ideas. Use **adverbials** – for example, 'furthermore', 'therefore', 'significantly', 'on the other hand' – to signpost the direction your writing is taking.

Revision Guide Page 75

Hint

When you add detail to your ideas, think about your **audience**. What information will they need? What is their view on the topic likely to be? If you think they might oppose your ideas, use **counter-arguments** to point out why they are wrong.

Revision Guide Page 56

Hint

Use a range of appropriate **rhetorical devices** to engage your audience. Think about rhetorical questions, direct address, repetition, lists, alliteration and hyperbole, for example.

Revision Guide Page 56

Watch out!

Take care not to overuse **rhetorical devices** – think about where they will be most effective. Rather than using a list of devices think about whether they are appropriate. For example, a rhetorical question can be an effective way to establish your point of view or challenge the audience; repetition can emphasise a key point, as long as the word or phrase you are repeating has real impact.

Revision Guide Pages 27–28 and 56

Hint

Vary the way you start your sentences for effect. For example, with: a **pronoun** (I, we); an article (the, a); a **preposition** (above, behind); an **'ing' word** (running, hurrying); an **adjective** (slow, quiet); an **adverb** (happily, quickly); a **conjunction** (if, although).

Revision Guide Page 88

Aim higher

Use a **wide range of ambitious vocabulary** and choose your words for impact. For example, using emotive language is a way of shaping your audience's response.

Revision Guide Pages 79–80

Watch out!

Don't rush your **conclusion**. Include ideas for the conclusion in your plan, and make sure it leaves your reader with a lasting impression. It can be used to sum up your ideas but avoid just repeating them. Instead, try to convey a clear final message.

Revision Guide Page 72

LEARN IT!

Use **apostrophes** correctly in **contractions** (don't, hasn't) and to show **possession** (the charity's donations, the fundraisers' efforts).

Revision Guide Page 93

Watch out!

Apostrophes are not used to indicate that a noun is plural – for example, the plural of carrot is carrots, not carrot's.

Hint

Always **check your work** carefully. Look out for spelling mistakes, missing or incorrect punctuation, and grammatical errors. Read it through slowly to ensure it makes sense.

Revision Guide Page 99

Paper 1: Explorations in creative reading and writing

Time allowed: 1 hour 45 minutes

There are 40 marks for Section A and 40 marks for Section B

The source that follows is:

Source A: 20th Century prose-fiction
Love for Lydia by H. E. Bates
It is an extract from a novel written in 1952, but set in the 1920s.

This extract is from the opening of the novel. The narrator, a young journalist, is describing his first sighting of Lydia Aspen, who arrives in his town with her two aunts, the Aspen sisters.

After the death of their elder brother the two Aspen sisters came back to Evensford at the end of February, driving in the enormous brown coachwork Daimler[1] with the gilt monograms[2] on the doors, through a sudden fall of snow.

Across the valley the floods of January, frozen to wide lakes of ice, were cut into enormous rectangular patterns by black hedgerows that lay like a wreckage of logs washed down on the broken river. A hard dark wind blew straight across the ice from the north-east, beating in at that end of the town where for a few hundred yards the High Street runs straight, past what is now Johnson's car-wrecking yard, under the railway arches, and then between the high causeways that make it like a dry canal. It was so cold that solid ice seemed to be whipped up from the valley on the wind, to explode into whirlwinds of harsh and bitter dust that pranced about in stinging clouds. Ice formed everywhere in dry black pools, polished in sheltered places, ruckled with dark waves at street corners or on sloping gutters where wind had flurried the last falls of rain.

Frost had begun in the third week of January, and from that date until the beginning of April it did not leave us for a day. All the time the same dark wind came with it, blowing bitterly and savagely over long flat meadows of frozen floods. There was no snow with it until the afternoon the Aspen sisters came back; and then it began to fall lightly, in sudden flusters, no more than vapour, and then gritty and larger, like grains of rice.

It began falling almost exactly at the moment the heavy brown Daimler drove past the old Succoth chapel, with its frozen steps like a waterfall of chipped glass, opposite the branch offices of *The County Examiner*[3], where the windows were partly glazed over with a pattern of starry fern. It came suddenly on a darkened whirl of wind that flowered into whiteness. The wind seemed to twist violently in the air and snatch from nowhere the snow that was like white vapour, catching the Daimler broadside[4] at the same time. Through the windows of *The Examiner*, where I stood nursing the wrist I had sprained while skating, I saw the car shudder and swerve and twist itself into a skid and then out again. From a confusion of leopard rugs on the back seat the younger Miss Aspen, Juliana, seemed to shudder too and was swung forward, snatching at the silken window cord with her right hand. The elder one, Bertie, bounced like a rosy dumpling. They were still both in black. But round the neck of the younger one was pinned a violet woollen scarf, as if she had caught a cold, and it was when she jolted forward, clutching the scarf with one hand and the window cord with the other, that I saw Elliott Aspen's daughter, Lydia, sitting there, between her aunts, for the first time.

She had long coils of black hair that fell across her shoulders, so that she seemed to be wearing a hood. I saw only part of her face, jerked forward above her raised coat collar, startled but not frightened by the skid. She did not lift her hands. It was her eyes instead that seemed to stretch out, first to one window and then another, in an effort to get her bearings, as if she did not know exactly where she was. And in that moment, before the car straightened and righted itself and went on, she seemed, I thought, about fifteen.

It was my first mistake about her.

[1]*Daimler – a large, luxurious and very expensive car*
[2]*monograms – sets of a person's initials*
[3]*The County Examiner – the local newspaper where the narrator works*
[4]*broadside – on the side (i.e. on the side of the Daimler)*

Set B
Paper 1

Time

Before you answer any questions, spend about **15 minutes reading** the source and all five questions you have to answer (in Section A and Section B).

After the reading time, spend about **45 minutes on Section A** – including planning and checking time – and about **5 minutes on Question 1**.

Unlocking the question

Underline the key words in the question before you begin writing so that you are sure about the **focus** of the question.

Hint

You don't need to use full sentences to answer Question 1. Just identify the information in the source and list your points.

Revision Guide
Pages 13–14

Watch out!

Stick closely to the focus of the question. Here you are being asked about the sisters' **journey**.

Watch out!

Don't just copy out the section the question is asking about! Keep any quotations as short as possible and make sure you copy them correctly.

SECTION A – Reading

Answer ALL questions in this section.

You are advised to spend about 45 minutes on this section.

1 Read again the first part of the source from **lines 1 to 2**.
List **four** things from this part of the source about the Aspen sisters' journey.

(4 marks)

1 ....

....

2 ....

....

3 ....

....

4 ....

....

2 Look in detail at this extract from **lines 7 to 14** of the source:

> It was so cold that solid ice seemed to be whipped up from the valley on the wind, to explode into whirlwinds of harsh and bitter dust that pranced about in stinging clouds. Ice formed everywhere in dry black pools, polished in sheltered places, ruckled with dark waves at street corners or on sloping gutters where wind had flurried the last falls of rain.
>
> Frost had begun in the third week of January, and from that date until the beginning of April it did not leave us for a day. All the time the same dark wind came with it, blowing bitterly and savagely over long flat meadows of frozen floods. There was no snow with it until the afternoon the Aspen sisters came back; and then it began to fall lightly, in sudden flusters, no more than vapour, and then gritty and larger, like grains of rice.

How does the writer use language here to describe the weather?
You could include the writer's choice of:
- words and phrases
- language features and techniques
- sentence forms.

(8 marks)

Time

Spend about **10 minutes** on this question.

Unlocking the question

The bullet points remind you that this question is testing your ability to comment on how **language** and **structure** are used for **effect**. You don't have to cover all of the bullet points – focus on the ones that are most relevant to the extract.

Unlocking the question

Underline the key words in the question first so that you understand the **focus**. Here, the focus is the language used to describe the weather, so you should look at descriptive words, phrases and techniques.

Watch out!

Don't just identify every interesting language feature – always start by focusing on the question. Read through the extract carefully, underlining words and phrases that relate to the question.

Watch out!

Don't just label sentences as single-clause (simple), multi-clause (compound and complex) or minor. Make sure you comment on **why** they have been used and the **effects** they create.

Revision Guide
Pages 31–32

Hint

As well as looking at **figurative language**, always consider the writer's **vocabulary** choices. Use inference to think of the **connotations** of individual words and phrases – but remember to stay focused on the question!

Revision Guide
Pages 19–21

LEARN IT!

Make sure you are familiar with a wide range of **language techniques, figurative language devices** and **word classes**. Here, for example, you could look out for adjectives, personification, metaphors and similes, lists and adverbs.

Revision Guide
Pages 19–23

Watch out!

Don't just list the techniques and devices you find – you must **explain their effect in relation to the question focus.** You can still explain the connotations or effects even if you don't know the name of the technique or device being used.

3 You now need to think about the **whole** of the source.

This text is taken from the opening of a novel.

How has the writer structured the text to interest you as a reader?

You could write about:
- what the writer focuses your attention on at the beginning
- how and why the writer changes this focus as the source develops
- any other structural features that interest you.

(8 marks)

Time

Spend about **10 minutes** on this question.

Unlocking the question

The question will remind you about where in a novel or story the extract has come from – here, it is from the opening of a novel. Use this information as a starting point when you consider structure. For example, does the opening plunge the reader straight into dramatic action, or is the pace slower and more descriptive?

Hint

When you look at structure, it is often a good idea to start with the **opening** of the extract. This may set the scene, or introduce a character. Some openings set up questions or puzzles to create tension or excitement for the reader.

Revision Guide page 29

Watch out!

Remember to back up all of your points with **evidence** from the source. You can use short, embedded quotations or paraphrase the text.

Revision Guide Page 37

Hint

Always consider the **pace** of the writing. For example, this source starts slowly with a detailed description of the icy weather. The slow pace is maintained – at the end, a whole paragraph is used to describe Lydia Aspen.

Watch out!

This question asks you about structure. Be careful not to slip into language analysis – **stick to structural features** and make sure you cover the **whole** of the source.

LEARN IT!

Make sure you are familiar with a **wide range of structural features**, including: sequencing, shifts in pace or focus, paragraph links, repetition of ideas, narrative voice, and the withholding of information.

Revision Guide Page 24

Watch out!

The source you are given is unlikely to include every possible structural feature. Don't just list every feature you find. Identify the ones that are **relevant** to the question, then **explain their effects**.

4 Focus this part of your answer on the second part of the source from **line 15 to the end**.

A student, having read this section of the text, said: 'The writer builds a real sense of drama before introducing Lydia Aspen. This makes you really appreciate why the narrator finds her so fascinating.'

To what extent do you agree?

In your response, you could:

- write about your own impressions of Lydia Aspen's arrival
- evaluate how the writer has created these impressions
- support your opinions with references to the text.

(20 marks)

....

....

....

....

....

....

....

....

....

....

....

....

....

....

....

....

....

....

....

....

....

....

....

....

....

....

....

Time

Spend about **20 minutes** on this question – **5 minutes planning**, and **15 minutes writing**.

Unlocking the question

The statement in the question might focus on different aspects of the source – for example, the writer's creation of character, setting, mood or atmosphere. Here, the statement refers to 'a real sense of drama' – so the focus is on the **mood** of the source.

Unlocking the question

Find and underline the sections of the source that relate to the question. Then use inference to assess the effect these aspects would have on the reader. Remember to evaluate **how** the writer has achieved the effects. Here, for example, you could look at the descriptions of the wind, the ice, and the car swerving, and consider **how** they create drama.

Revision Guide

Pages 15 and 35–36

Hint

You could draw a box around the lines in the source that you need to look at. This will help you to **focus on the correct text**.

Hint

Use the statement given in the question as a clear focus for your evaluation. Consider **how far** you agree with the statement – but remember you can still give your own opinions, **backed up with supporting evidence.**

Revision Guide Page 37

Watch out!

Don't just re-tell the story in your own words. Remember to comment on your own impressions and on **how** these effects are created – the **methods** the writer uses.

LEARN IT!

Use **explanatory phrases** to structure your answer, for example: The writer makes…, The reader might feel…, When we read this, we feel…, We are encouraged by the writer to…

Watch out!

You need to evaluate the effect on the reader, but you should avoid criticising the extract. **Focus on making positive judgements about the effect of the text on the reader.**

SECTION B – Writing
You are advised to spend about 45 minutes on this section.
Write in full sentences.
You are reminded of the need to plan your answer.
You should leave enough time to check your work at the end.

5 You are going to enter a creative writing competition.

Your entry will be judged by a panel of people of your own age.

Either: Write a description suggested by this picture:

Or: Write the opening part of a story about meeting somebody for the first time.

(24 marks for content and organisation
16 marks for technical accuracy)
(40 marks)

....

....

....

....

....

....

....

....

....

....

....

....

Time

Spend about **45 minutes** on Section B – for example, **5 minutes planning**, **35 minutes writing**, **5 minutes checking** your work.

Unlocking the question

You will be given a **choice of two writing tasks** but you only need to **answer one**. You might have a choice between one description and one narrative task, two description tasks, or two narrative tasks.

Unlocking the question

The question might give you an idea of your **audience**. Always check to see if this is the case. Here, for example, your writing will need to appeal to, and be appropriate for, 'a panel of people of your own age'.

Watch out!

Pay attention to content, organisation and technical accuracy – spelling, punctuation and grammar! Your writing for Section B will be marked against all these points. Save five minutes to check your work when you've finished writing and proofread it for mistakes.

Revision Guide
Pages 96–99

Hint

Make a plan before you start writing. If you are writing a description, try imagining yourself in the scene – then, think about what you can see, who you are with and what is happening.

Revision Guide Page 65

Hint

If you are writing a story, plan a simple structure with – as relevant – a **clear beginning, middle and end**.

Revision Guide Page 66

Watch out!

Read both of the question options carefully. Here, the second option only asks for the **opening part** of a story – so you could just plan the beginning and perhaps the middle of a narrative.

Aim higher

To make your narrative structure more exciting for the reader, think about using techniques such as **flashback**. Start with a tense or dramatic event, then go back in time to describe how it happened.

Aim higher

If you are only writing the opening part of a story, you could end at a point of **tension**, using a **cliffhanger** technique.

Watch out!

Remember to use paragraphs to structure your writing. Usually, you should start a new paragraph each time you start a new point – but shorter paragraphs can be used carefully for effect.

Revision Guide Page 74

LEARN IT!

Learn the spellings of common **homophones** (words that sound the same), such as: your/you're, there/their/they're, to/too/two, allowed/aloud, we're/where/wear/were, of/off, past/passed and our/are.

Watch out!

Avoid the common mistake of writing 'would of' instead of 'would have'. Make sure you use **would have**, **could have** and **should have** – not would of, could of or should of.

Revision Guide Page 96

LEARN IT!

Use apostrophes correctly in **contractions**. The apostrophe should go in place of the missing letter or letters: cannot = can't, do not = don't, I will = I'll.

Revision Guide Page 93

Hint

Don't clutter your writing with too many events or unnecessary characters. Short stories work best when they have just one or two main characters and just one main event. Concentrate on developing your characters rather than adding complicated action scenes.

Watch out!

Be careful how you end sentences. **Avoid a comma splice** – when you join two sentences with a comma (The dog barked, he was hungry.). Instead, use a full stop to separate them (The dog barked. He was hungry.) or a conjunction (The dog barked because he was hungry.).

Revision Guide Page 91

Aim higher

Brackets can be used in pairs to add information that isn't essential to your main point. For example: 'My mother (shouting as usual) refused to let me go.' Here, the brackets hint that the narrator has a difficult relationship with her mother.

Revision Guide Page 94

LEARN IT!

Make sure you **punctuate dialogue correctly**. Enclose the words that are spoken within speech marks. Don't forget to include punctuation just before the closing speech marks.

Revision Guide Page 93

Hint

If you are writing a whole short story, you could divide your writing time into three ten-minute chunks: ten minutes on the beginning, ten minutes on the plot development in the middle, and ten minutes on the ending. Stop after each section and check that what you have written makes sense.

LEARN IT!

Learn and revise words with **tricky spellings**, such as necessary, definitely and separately. Make a list of the ones you regularly get wrong and practise spelling them correctly.

Revision Guide Pages 96–98

Hint

Always save five minutes to **check your work** when you've finished writing. Look out for changes in tense, spelling errors, missing words, and missing or incorrect punctuation.

Revision Guide Page 99

Paper 2: Writers' viewpoints and perspectives

Time allowed: 1 hour 45 minutes

There are 40 marks for Section A and 40 marks for Section B

The sources that follow are:

Source A: 21st Century non-fiction
'Parenting: Marty Poppins is taking charge in the nursery' by Roland White
An extract from a newspaper article about male nannies, published in 2004.

Source B: 19th Century literary non-fiction
'A New Occupation for Girls' by Rosa Nouchette Carey
An extract from a magazine published in 1893.

Please turn the page over to see the sources

Source A – 21st Century non-fiction

Roland White writes about male nannies in this extract from an article published in *The Sunday Times* in 2004.

Parenting: Marty Poppins[1] is taking charge in the nursery

The Sunday Times, 18 July 2004

Peter Cummins, the first man to graduate from Norland College[2], the august[3] school for nannies, tells Roland White that childcare is easy work.

Easy work until now, that is. The first British male nanny has just graduated from the college in Bath. Peter Cummins, 21, is a former schoolboy rugby prop[4] who hadn't a clue what he fancied doing with his life. He decided he wanted to be a nanny after working as a male au pair[5] on a gap-year[6] trip to France.

"I ended up looking after a family with six children near Lyons and had a great time," he says. "I liked reading stories to the children — in French, of course — and being corrected every so often."

If you are a parent trying to juggle your career and your children, you will like the sound of Peter. He is happy to work non-stop from 7am until bedtime stories at 8pm. He is careful to load the dishwasher after meals and to clean the floor of cake crumbs and yoghurt. And this is the best bit: he doesn't even think it's particularly hard work. "It certainly doesn't feel like hard work," he says. "Although at the end of the day you do feel tired."

Peter, from Ceredigion, west Wales, pressed ahead with nanny training despite being warned by a careers adviser that the childcare profession was dominated by women: recent figures show that men form only 2% of the workforce. He was the only male at a nursery placement, the only male at a primary school where he did work experience, and — for the past two years — the only male among the 70 students at Norland.

"I don't see any problem," he says. "My careers adviser hinted that it was very female-dominated, but I took no notice."

As part of his two-year course, Peter spent every other week on work experience. He also did a fortnight with Simon and Heather Call, of Bath, looking after their three children, two boys aged two and four and a 10-month-old girl. "We thought a male nanny would be a good role model for the boys, and that's how it turned out," says Simon. "He played really energetic games with them and really got his hands dirty." Peter spent his days making paper airplanes, foot painting and playing football, croquet and hide and seek in the garden.

The government has been trying to attract more men into childcare and has a target level of 6%, but even this small improvement looks quite ambitious. The Daycare Trust, a childcare charity, launched a recruitment campaign last year under the slogan "He Who Cares Wins"[7] but a spokesman admitted last week: "There was evidence of an increase in calls to the education department recruitment lines, but it's a very long-term aim."

Female domination of the nanny business is so complete that the two main lavatories at Norland are marked "Ladies" and "Ladies". The gents is down in the basement somewhere. And Peter had to have all the feminine wording on his certificate altered to "he" and "him". Even then a couple of "shes" still slipped through. Although Norland nannies are famed for their uniforms, there is no male equivalent. For a formal event on the last day of term, Peter had to wear a suit.

Luckily, wearing uniforms at work is now a rare event. "Most people these days don't want to draw attention to their children," says Rebekah Yeomans, of Norland. "But we still have one family in the UK — members of the nobility — who insist that their staff wear uniforms."

After two years at Norland College, Peter has a 20-page list of jobs for which he can apply but for a year he will be a probationer[8], still supervised by Norland. During this time he will be expected to live with his family and can earn up to £550 a week. If he later gets a job overseas he can expect to earn up to £1,200 a week. He'll need the money: training at Norland costs £2,895 a term for six terms.

[1]*Marty Poppins – a word-play on the fictional nanny Mary Poppins, made famous in the 1964 film of the same name*
[2]*Norland College – the most famous and expensive childcare college in the UK*
[3]*august – respected and impressive*
[4]*prop – a very strong and muscular member of a rugby team*
[5]*au pair – a young person who lives with a family in a foreign country and helps with homework and childcare in return for a room, food and pocket money*
[6]*gap-year – a year 'off' between finishing school and starting university*
[7]*"He Who Cares Wins" – a word-play on the motto of the SAS (Special Air Service), 'Who Dares Wins'*
[8]*probationer – someone serving a trial period in a job*

Source B – 19th Century literary non-fiction

This is an extract from an article published in *The Girl's Own Paper* in 1893. *The Girl's Own Paper* was a Victorian magazine aimed at girls and young women. This article is about the Norland Institute (now called Norland College), which opened in 1892 to train young women to become nannies and which the writer has recently visited.

A New Occupation for Girls

'The object of the Institute is', the prospectus[1] tells us, 'to supply the public with ladies as trained nurses for young children, and to form a new occupation for young women whose circumstances do not enable them to undergo the long course of professional training now essential to a successful educational career, even when they are endowed with sufficiently good intellectual abilities'.

The scheme of training extends over nine months, and the course of training in the Institute comprises instruction in needlework, hygiene, and useful knowledge. Practical lessons are given on the making of beef-tea, etc., the preparation of poultices[2], and simple remedies for cuts, burns, and sprains.

The fees for six months' training inclusive of three months' residence in the Institute, board, washing, uniform, teaching, materials, apparatus, necessary fees at hospital, amount to £36. The minimum salary for a nurse is £20 for the first year, with an annual rise of £2 for the next four years.

The rules for employer and employed are very simple – the nurse is not expected to scrub floors nor carry coals, not to take her meals with any servant, except the nursery maid, and she is entitled to a month's holiday in the year.

This admirable Institute (which is, of course, in its infancy, having only been started a few months ago) has at present only twelve probationers[3] some of whom are undergoing their hospital training; but as Miss Sharman, the Principal, informed us, it is just in time to supply an increasing future need.

What especially struck me after a little unrestrained talk with the girls, was their evident enthusiasm and engrossing interest in their future work; to them it was above all things a labour of love; they were eager young crusaders[4], ready with a will to tread the new untried paths of womanly independence.

My attention was attracted to a delicate-looking girl, who seemed to me, from her youthful appearance, to be hardly up to the requisite age for probationer – eighteen to thirty are the limits.

'Surely you are not eighteen,' I ventured to say; but was amused by her energetic answer. She was eighteen, she informed me, with a touch of womanly pride, and had had the sole care of a baby of four months. Again I hazarded an unfortunate observation when I asked her if she did not find that carrying an infant was a strain on her strength. 'Not at all,' was her decided reply, 'she did not mind it in the least', and I took home a lesson to myself, not to judge too much from outward appearance.

By-and-by a bright, merry-looking girl came down to show herself. She had put on the new uniform for our inspection, and a very pretty uniform it was. The dress was cornflower blue beige, doubtless wonderfully becoming to bright complexions and fair hair; and we were told pink galatea[5] was the morning working dress – little crimped frills and tie, but no cap.

The length of the dress was anxiously debated. 'It must not be too long,' said the Principal, 'because you will have to play with the children, and they will trample on you.' And when one looked at those bright young faces, one felt that they would play with the children many a merry game.

Difficulties will come; no road on earth is free from thorns, no work without need of patience, and our young probationers will doubtless have their trials. Employers and employed will have to learn to know each other, and to work together happily.

[1]prospectus – a printed booklet giving details of what a school or university offers
[2]poultices – a mixture including bran, flour and herbs, which is applied to the body to reduce swelling and kept in place with a cloth
[3]probationers – people serving a trial period in a job
[4]crusaders – someone who believes strongly in something and does all they can to achieve it
[5]galatea – a strong cotton material

SECTION A – Reading

Answer ALL questions in this section.

You are advised to spend about 45 minutes on this section.

1 Read again the first part of **Source A** from **lines 1 to 13**.
Choose **four** statements below which are TRUE.

- Shade the **circles** in the boxes of the ones that you think are true.
- Choose a maximum of four statements.
- If you make an error cross out the **whole box**.
- If you change your mind and require a statement that has been crossed out then draw a circle around the box.

(4 marks)

A Peter Cummins is the first male nanny to graduate from a London college. ○

B Peter Cummins played rugby when he was at school. ○

C Peter Cummins travelled the world on a gap year. ○

D Peter Cummins enjoyed working as a male au pair. ○

E Nannies may need to work long hours. ○

F Peter Cummins was the only student from Wales at Norland. ○

G Before training as a nanny, Peter Cummins took career advice. ○

H Only 2% of the students at Norland are male. ○

Time

Before you answer any questions, spend about **15 minutes reading** the sources and all five questions you have to answer (in Section A and Section B).

Time

Don't spend too long on this question. After the reading time, spend about **45 minutes on Section A** – including planning and checking time – and about **5 minutes on Question 1**.

Watch out!

Make sure you select **only four statements**.

Hint

Read all the statements carefully before you mark your answers. If you skim read them too quickly, some incorrect answers may seem correct.

Revision Guide
Pages 13–15

Watch out!

Each true statement you identify for this answer is only worth **one mark** – so do not spend too long on your answer.

Time

Spend about **8 minutes** on this question.

Unlocking the question

Always **read the question carefully** before you start your answer. **Underline key words** so that you are sure about what details you need to find in the sources.

Unlocking the question

This question is only worth 8 marks. It will have a specific focus – here, the differences between Peter and the nannies in Source B – so there may not be many possible points to include.

Watch out!

Only identify and select **information that is relevant** to the question. For example, this question asks you about the differences between the male nanny in Source A and the nannies in Source B – any other differences between the sources are not relevant.

2 You need to refer to **Source A** and **Source B** for this question.

Both sources are about nannies.

Use details from **both** sources to write a summary of the differences between Peter Cummins and the nannies described in Source B.

(8 marks)

Hint

When you write your answer, make a point about one source and then add a related comment about the other source in the same paragraph. This will help you to make sure you **refer to both sources** in your synthesis.

Revision Guide Pages 39–41

Hint

You need to use details from the sources as **evidence** to support your ideas. These textual references can be **quotations** or you can **paraphrase** the text. Keep quotations brief and accurate, and if you paraphrase take care not to change the meaning.

LEARN IT!

Make sure you know a wide variety of phrases that show you are using **inference** in your answer. For example: This suggests…, This might suggest…, This shows…, This implies…, You could infer from this…

Revision Guide Page 15

Watch out!

Always make it clear which source you are writing about – either by using the writer's name, or by calling them 'Source A' and 'Source B'.

Time

Spend about **12 minutes** on this question.

Unlocking the question

To answer successfully:

- stick closely to the **question focus** throughout your answer
- show that you understand the **effects** of the language used
- use **evidence** from the **correct lines** of the source text
- use **accurate subject terminology** where possible.

Revision Guide Page 16

Hint

When you write about sentence types, you don't need to quote full sentences. Just make it clear which sentence you are writing about. For example, 'The writer uses a long list to present the wide variety of activities that Peter's role involves. This emphasises...'

Hint

Pay attention to titles and sub-headings when you look at language. Look out for word-play throughout, too. Here, the play on the SAS motto in the slogan 'He Who Cares Wins' helps to emphasise that childcare is an unusual profession for men.

3 You now need to refer **only** to **Source A** from **lines 16 to 29**.
How does the writer use language to show that Peter is an unusual nanny?

(12 marks)

....

....

....

....

....

....

....

....

....

....

....

....

....

....

....

....

....

....

....

....

....

....

....

....

....

....

....

....

....

....

....

Hint

You don't have to fill all the writing lines provided – they are just a guide. But if you always need more paper for this question, you may be writing too much.

Hint

Aim to make **at least three** clear points in your answer. Make sure you support them with evidence from the source and that you analyse and explain the effects of the language choices you identify.

Hint

Look out for any interesting or advanced punctuation – such as dashes – and their effects.

Hint

Use **short, embedded quotations** where possible. Always use quotation marks and make sure you copy the quotations down correctly from the source.

LEARN IT!

Some of the skills you need for Paper 2 are the same as for Paper 1. For example, on Paper 2 you can still use **inference** and think about the **connotations** of different words and phrases – in Source A, you might look at the connotations of language like 'dominated'.

Revision Guide
Pages 15 and 20

Time

Spend about **20 minutes** on this question – about **5 minutes planning**, and **15 minutes writing**.

Unlocking the question

Use the bullet points in the question to focus your answer: '**attitudes**' means **ideas and perspectives**; '**methods**' means the **language and structural techniques** the writers use.

Revision Guide Pages 39, 42–48

Hint

You must read both sources and make a plan before you start writing. This will help you to structure an effective answer and will mean you are less likely to miss important points.

Hint

Start with the writers' ideas and perspectives. Skim read both texts to make sure you understand the writers' main ideas and how they both feel about the topic. Here, for example, the writer of Source A describes Peter Cummins as a 'former schoolboy rugby prop', which may suggest a particular attitude towards male nannies.

Revision Guide Page 46

4 For this question, you need to refer to the **whole of Source A**, together with the **whole of Source B**.

Compare how the writers convey their different attitudes to childcare and being a nanny.

In your answer, you could:

- compare their different attitudes
- compare the methods they use to convey their attitudes
- support your response with references to both texts.

(16 marks)

Watch out!

Your answer **must** focus on **how** the writers convey their ideas and perspectives, so make sure you **compare their methods**. Look for similarities as well as differences.

Hint

Structure your comparison clearly. First, give a short overview of the sources and their purposes. Next, make a point about Source A, give evidence and comment on the writer's method. Then do the same with a comparative point about Source B. Then go on to make another point about Source A, and so on.

Revision Guide Page 48

Watch out!

Make sure you stay focused on the question throughout your answer.

Hint

Always make it clear which source you are referring to – either by using the writers' names, or by calling them 'Source A' and 'Source B'. This will make your answer easier to follow.

Watch out!

Make sure you stay focused on the **attitudes of the writers** – don't start discussing the attitudes of people the writer is writing about!

Hint

Consider the language features the writers use – for example, word classes (nouns, verbs, adjectives, adverbs), and rhetorical and language techniques such as direct address, repetition, expert evidence and lists.

Revision Guide Pages 12, 19, 27–28

Watch out!

Don't spend too long on one point – you need to **cover a range of ideas** in your answer.

Hint

Don't forget to consider structural features. For example, you could compare the way the sources start and end, or the order in which they sequence their ideas.

Revision Guide Page 30

Watch out!

The 19th-century text may contain some ideas that seem unfashionable or even unpleasant to a modern reader. But don't just say that it is 'old-fashioned' – think about what this suggests about the attitudes of the writer. Take care: **your focus needs to be on comparing the sources**, so only comment on these ideas and attitudes if it's part of a comparative point you are making about the two texts.

LEARN IT!

Make sure you are familiar with **a wide range of text forms and purposes**: for example, biographies, articles, letters, speeches and reports.

Revision Guide
Pages 61–63

Time

Spend about **45 minutes** on Section B – for example, **5 minutes planning**, **35 minutes writing**, **5 minutes checking** your work.

Unlocking the question

The writing question will be on a similar topic to the reading sources in Section A, so you could use these texts to generate ideas. However, **your answer must be your own work** – if you do take ideas from the reading sources, only use a few key points and develop them to make them your own – don't just copy the text into your answer.

Watch out!

Pay attention to content, organisation and technical accuracy – spelling, punctuation and grammar! Your writing for Section B will be marked against all these points. Save five minutes to check your work when you've finished writing and proofread it for mistakes.

Revision Guide
Pages 96–99

SECTION B – Writing

You are advised to spend about 45 minutes on this section.

You are reminded of the need to plan your answer.

You should write in full sentences.

You should leave enough time to check your work at the end.

5 'Schools are still pushing students into traditional gender roles. This is wrong – men are more than capable of childcare and women should be inspired to go into careers like engineering or science.'

Write the text of a speech for an event at your school or college in which you persuade young people of your own age to agree with your point of view on this statement.

(24 marks for content and organisation
16 marks for technical accuracy)

(40 marks)

Hint

Make a plan before you start writing – for example, a spider diagram or a list of bullet points. Include ideas for about five or six paragraphs. You can agree or disagree with the statement in the question. For this question you might agree that all careers should be open to both genders. Just remember that all your points will need to be developed with detail such as expert opinions, anecdotes or facts and statistics.

Revision Guide
Pages 69–70

Watch out!

If you use a spider diagram to plan your answer, make sure you **number your points**. This will help you to structure your answer in a clear sequence.

Hint

Include ideas for your **introduction** in your plan. Aim to make your opening as engaging as possible, but make sure it suits your audience and purpose.

Revision Guide
Pages 69–70

Watch out!

Stay focused on the question throughout your answer. Making a plan before you start writing will help you with this.

LEARN IT!

Learn and revise words with **tricky spellings**, such as necessary, definitely and separately. Make a list of the ones you regularly get wrong and practise spelling them correctly.

Revision Guide
Pages 96–98

Watch out!

Be careful with **capital letters**. You must use one at the start of each sentence and for all proper nouns, such as the name Kareem.

Hint

Choose the **language devices** and the **words** you use with care. Think about the **connotations** of your vocabulary choices and the effect they will have on your audience.

Revision Guide
Pages 19–20, 27–28

Hint

Use a range of **structural features** that are appropriate for the form of your writing. Examples include headings and subheadings, introductions, different types and lengths of sentences, and conclusions.

Revision Guide
Pages 61–63

Hint

Use a range of **punctuation**, but especially **commas**. These can be used to separate clauses in a sentence (for example, 'The house, which dominated the skyline, was still and silent as I approached.') or to separate items in a list (for example, 'I felt empty, cold and alone.').

Revision Guide Page 92

Watch out!

Be careful how you end sentences. **Avoid a comma splice** – when you join two sentences with a comma (The dog barked, he was hungry.). Instead, use a full stop to separate them (The dog barked. He was hungry.) or a conjunction (The dog barked because he was hungry.).

Revision Guide Page 91

Aim higher

Consider advanced punctuation. For example: **brackets** can be used in pairs to add information in a humorous way; **colons** can introduce an example, a list or an explanation.

Revision Guide Page 94

Hint

If you are using **expert evidence, facts or statistics** in your writing, you can make them up – as long as they are believable and relevant to the point you are making.

Revision Guide Page 12

Watch out!

Take care to punctuate any quotations you include correctly. Use **quotation marks** to enclose the words you are quoting.

LEARN IT!

Build up a bank of **synonyms** for words that you use regularly in your writing. For example, instead of repeating the word 'idea', you could use opinion, viewpoint, notion or concept.

Revision Guide Page 79

Aim higher

To create an informal tone, try using **colloquial idioms** – everyday phrases with particular meanings that aren't directly related to the individual words, such as 'the penny dropped' (meaning someone suddenly realises something). Make sure any idioms you use are appropriate for your audience.

Hint

Always **check your work** carefully. Look out for spelling mistakes, missing or incorrect punctuation, and grammatical errors. Read it through slowly to ensure it makes sense.

Revision Guide Page 99

SECTION A – Reading
Answer ALL questions in this section.
You are advised to spend about 45 minutes on this section.

1 Read again the first part of the source from **lines 1 to 4**.
List **four** things from this part of the source about the woods.

(4 marks)

1 The woods had a track

2 'The birds were astir'

3 There were butterflies

4 There were bees

Quotation is kept short and relevant.

Hint

Turn to page 1 to re-read the source.

All pieces of information listed are from the lines given in the question – this shows that the student has read both the question and section of the source carefully.

Good use of paraphrase that does not change the meaning of the source.

Alternative answers

Answers to Question 1 could also include:

- the air was warm
- there was a 'glimmer of water'.

Hint

Read the notes below, then look at the sample answer on page 67.

2 Look in detail at this extract from **lines 8 to 16** of the source:

> The tide was ebbing, the water oozing away from the mud flats, and here, where she stood, was the head of the creek itself, for the stream ended in a trickle, and the trickle in a spring. The creek twisted round a belt of trees, and she began to walk along the bank, happy, fascinated, forgetting her mission, for this discovery was a pleasure quite unexpected, this creek was a source of enchantment, a new escape, better than Navron itself, a place to drowse and sleep, a lotus-land. There was a heron, standing in the shallows, solemn and grey, his head sunk in his hooded shoulders, and beyond him a little oyster-catcher pattered in the mud, and then, weird and lovely, a curlew called and, rising from the bank, flew away from her down the creek. Something, not herself, disturbed the birds, for the heron rose slowly, flapping his slow wings, and followed the curlew, and Dona paused a moment, for she too had heard a sound, a sound of tapping, of hammering.

How does the writer use language here to describe the creek?
You could include the writer's choice of:
- words and phrases
- language features and techniques
- sentence forms.

(8 marks)

Writing a good answer

Good answers will include:

- analysis of the effects of the **language** chosen by the writer
- carefully selected (short) quotations or close reference to the text to back up the points being made
- sophisticated and accurate use of subject terminology.

Possible language points:

- Verbs are used to create the impression of a peaceful atmosphere – 'ebbing', 'oozing'.
- The repetition of 'trickle' suggests the place is peaceful and slow, as even the water is gentle and quiet.
- The verb 'twisted' creates a sense of danger/suspense.
- The adjectives used to describe Dona's mood – 'happy', 'fascinated' – have connotations of a welcome discovery.
- The noun 'discovery' has connotations of something new/unusual/unspoiled.
- The abstract noun 'enchantment', together with the noun 'escape', suggests something magical.
- The verb 'drowse' enhances the magical mood.
- The compound noun 'lotus-land' suggests peace, and somewhere idyllic/exotic.
- The list of birds associated with water support the realism of the setting and help to bring the scene to life for the reader.
- Multi-clause sentences build up a detailed image of the creek, engaging the reader.
- A build-up of verbs in the final sentences disrupts or breaks the calm atmosphere.
- The repetition of 'sound' in the final sentence breaks the tranquil mood and introduces an element of danger/ the unknown.

Clear use of Point – Evidence – Explain (P–E–E) to structure answer.

Concise opening paragraph that starts by accurately identifying the overall effect of a sentence form, then focuses on word choices and their specific effects, before ending with a link to the question focus.

Hint

Look at this sample answer to Question 2. Refer to the notes on page 66, then look to see how some of the points are used here.

Q2: sample answer

The opening complex sentence uses a series of clauses to build up a positive atmosphere. The verbs 'ebbing' and 'oozing' have connotations of something slowly fading, which together with the repetition of 'trickle' suggests the creek is a calm and peaceful place.

Another long, multi-clause sentence starting in line 9 is then used to build up a picture of somewhere unusual and perhaps slightly magical. The creek is described as 'twisted', which together with the nouns 'discovery', 'enchantment' and 'escape' suggests the creek is somewhere unspoiled. The sentence ends with the compound noun 'lotus-land', which has connotations of somewhere idyllic and slightly exotic.

A long, complex sentence describing the birds then starts to disrupt or break the calm of nature. The adjectives 'solemn and grey' carry connotations of something old and wise looking after the creek, but as the sentence progresses the calm is broken by verbs that increase in movement from 'sunk' to 'pattered', and then to 'rising'. In the final sentence, separate clauses are used to build up a sense of impending danger as the creek is 'disturbed' and the heron rises 'flapping his slow wings'. Finally, the verbs 'tapping' and 'hammering' are juxtaposed, creating the impression that something dangerous is about to happen.

Clear focus on the question.

Effects of sentence types considered.

Effects of a range of word classes considered.

Sophisticated use of subject terminology.

Connotations of word choices considered and explained in detail.

Shows understanding that the atmosphere changes within this short extract.

Detailed explanation of several language techniques.

Short, precise quotations embedded effectively in explanatory sentences.

Advanced use of subject terminology to explain a perceptive point about sentence forms.

Accurate use of subject terminology to make appropriate point about word choice.

A very strong answer because...

This is an analytical answer because it is concise, covers a range of word choices and language features, and clearly explains the effect of each piece of evidence. The student also uses some sophisticated subject terminology, such as 'compound noun' and 'juxtaposed'. The student identifies the change in atmosphere within the extract and refers to both sentence type and word choice to give a detailed explanation of the effect.

Quotations are short, relevant and embedded effectively into clear explanatory sentences.

Other examples of language features and techniques could also have been used. For example, the student could have mentioned the use of nouns to suggest something magical, or the adjectives that describe Dona's mood. However, this question is only worth 8 marks and it's not necessary (or possible, in the time available) to cover every possible language point in order to write a strong answer.

Hint

Read the notes below, then look at the sample answer on page 69.

3 You now need to think about the **whole** of the source.
This text is taken from an early chapter of a novel.
How has the writer structured the text to interest you as a reader?
You could write about:
- what the writer focuses your attention on at the beginning
- how and why the writer changes this focus as the source develops
- any other structural features that interest you.

(8 marks)

Writing a good answer

Good answers will include:

- analysis of the effects of the **structural** features chosen by the writer
- carefully selected (short) quotations or close reference to the text to back up the points being made
- sophisticated and accurate use of subject terminology.

Possible structural points:

- The source opens with a natural, calm, slightly magical scene.
- Overall structure – the writer takes the reader on a walk down to the creek, drawing the reader into the scene.
- The birds being 'disturbed' and the sound of 'hammering' foreshadows Dona's shock at the sight of the men on the ship.
- The creek is revealed slowly, creating a sense of peace but also anticipation for the reader.
- The focus shifts from the creek to the birds, reflecting Dona's enjoyment of the idyllic scene.
- The focus eventually narrows to the ship, creating a sense of tension.
- The focus shifts from the natural world (the creek) to something unnatural (the ship), introducing a sinister note for the reader.
- The narrative perspective moves from the general to the particular – from the ship, to the men, then to one man.
- The extract ends on a tense note as Dona listens, leaving the reader with a cliffhanger as Dona realises the man is singing in French.

Clear opening sentence that gives an overview of the effect of the structure.

Explanation of the effect of the opening, using relevant embedded quotations to support the point.

Hint

Look at this sample answer to Question 3. Refer back to the notes on page 68, then look to see how some of the points are used here.

Q3: sample answer

The extract opens with a natural, slightly magical scene, then takes the reader on a leisurely walk down to the creek before becoming tense when the focus is narrowed to the ship. There is a build-up of pleasant natural images such as the 'drowsy bumble bees' and the 'glimmer of water' in the woods, before the perspective is narrowed to Dona's view of the creek. The reader pauses with Dona to share her enjoyment of the idyllic scene. Each aspect of the creek is described in turn, from the 'belt of trees' to the birds, which are described individually, creating a slow pace and a peaceful atmosphere.

At the end of the first paragraph, there is the first hint that the atmosphere will change. The focus remains on the birds as 'something' disturbs them, and Dona hears 'hammering'. This foreshadows her discovery of the men on the ship.

The focus then shifts away from the natural to the sinister, as the ship is revealed slowly to the reader through Dona's eyes, creating a growing sense of tension and suspense. The focus then shifts further to the characters on the ship, starting with two men and then increasing the tension by closing in on one specific man, who is described as 'like a monkey'. At this point, the reader is taken inside Dona's head to experience her growing anxiety about the ship and its occupants. A final cliffhanger is created by her realisation that the man is singing in French.

Change in perspective identified.

Advanced explanatory phrase used to show understanding of effects.

Pace and atmosphere are considered.

Shows a detailed understanding of the way the focus shifts throughout the extract.

Sophisticated use of terminology shows perceptive understanding.

Shift of focus identified and its effect analysed.

Explanation extended to show detailed understanding.

Shows understanding of the shift in focus from setting to characters.

Uses sophisticated terminology to show perceptive understanding of the effect of the ending.

A very strong answer because...

This is a concise answer which still covers a wide range of structural features, including foreshadowing and shifts in narrative perspective. The student structures the response chronologically, following the order of the text. This is effective as it tracks the changes in focus and perspective throughout the source.

The change from a peaceful atmosphere to a tense one is also tracked effectively. The student's explanation of how this change is achieved – via a shift away from the natural surroundings to the men on the ship – is sophisticated.

Terminology is used correctly throughout. Quotations are short, relevant and embedded effectively into clear explanatory sentences. The student also uses some sophisticated explanatory phrases – such as 'takes the reader on a leisurely walk' and 'the reader pauses'.

Other examples of structural techniques could also have been used. For example, the student could have discussed the way that the source moves from the general to the particular. However, this question is only worth 8 marks and it's not necessary (or possible, in the time available) to cover every possible structural point in order to write a strong answer.

Hint

Read the notes below, then look at the sample answer on pages 71–72.

4 Focus this part of your answer on the second part of the source from **line 17 to the end.**
A student, having read this section of the text, said: 'The writer makes the scene with the ship seem exciting and slightly dangerous. It is as if you are there with Dona, seeing it with her eyes.'

To what extent do you agree?

In your response, you could:
- write about your own impressions of the scene on the ship
- evaluate how the writer has created these impressions
- support your opinions with references to the text.

(20 marks)

Writing a good answer

Good answers will include:
- detailed and critical **evaluation** of the effect on the reader
- a perceptive understanding of the writer's methods and their effects
- carefully selected and relevant textual detail as evidence for all points being made
- a clear and close focus on the question.

Possible evaluative points:
- Readers can relate to Dona's pause and instinctive withdrawal, as they are made to see the ship through her eyes.
- The ship is 'so close', suggesting Dona could be in danger.
- The ship is first linked with night, which associates it with danger.
- The description of the ship as 'red and golden' suggests it stands out, and makes it sound exciting.
- The mention of the 'setting sun' on the sea associates the ship with a sense of romance, and creates a sense of anticipation.
- Verbs and adverbs are used to create a sense of danger/tension – 'steeply', 'ran away', 'twisted', 'turned', 'running'.
- The verbs 'frothing and bubbling' suggest celebration/excitement.
- The first paragraph in this section ends on a cliffhanger – 'no one was in it' – creating a sense of mystery for the reader.
- The phrase 'drowsy stillness' creates a sense of anticipation/waiting.
- 'No one' is repeated again in Dona's thoughts, echoing the emptiness of the boat moored at the quay and reminding the reader she is alone.
- Dona's thoughts are shared, making the scene more intimate and personal and allowing the reader to feel her fear.
- The verb 'shrouded' has connotations of death/crime.
- The interesting simile – 'like a monkey' – has connotations of distant, exotic lands.
- References to growing volume – 'softly at first, then a little louder' – suggest that danger is getting closer.
- Dona is separate from the men, and unseen, which adds to the excitement and tension, and she is a lone woman coming across several unknown men, which adds a sense of danger.
- The revelation that the man is 'singing in French' has exotic/dangerous/foreign connotations for Dona.

Overview at start of answer uses key words from the statement in the question and shows full understanding of the extract.

An evaluative statement, which is backed up with a structural feature as evidence.

Hint

Look at this sample answer to Question 4. Refer back to the notes on page 70, then look to see how some of the points are used here.

Q4: sample answer

I strongly agree that the ship is made to seem exciting and slightly dangerous, as it is revealed slowly and the reader is made to see it through Dona's eyes. For example, a sense of tension is created for the reader as they are made to pause with Dona at the corner of the creek, and when she withdraws 'instinctively' the reader would feel suspense and assume she is frightened by what she has seen.

The writer then uses several clauses in a long sentence to make the reader wait and draw out the tension before revealing that what she sees is a ship at anchor. It is made to seem dangerous as it is 'so close' she could have 'tossed a biscuit' onto the deck. However, when it is revealed that Dona 'recognized' it from the night before, as a 'painted ship on the horizon', the reader might begin to think that she has gone to the creek to find it again. The description makes it sound like it was just out of reach, as if waiting for her.
The ship is described as 'red and golden' which suggests something exciting, and the fact that she saw it in the 'setting sun' associates it with romance, perhaps making the reader think that she has gone back because she is attracted by the sense of adventure the ship represents.

A sense of excitement is emphasised as the ship is said to be in 'deep water' and the adverb 'steeply', used to describe the rise of the banks either side, suggests the occupants are brave and daring as they will obviously struggle to get ashore. The verbs 'frothing and bubbling' create a slightly celebratory feel which contrasts with the verb 'twisted' to describe the creek, perhaps encouraging the reader to see the ship as exciting, but out of place and therefore dangerous.

Short, embedded quotations are used to support points.

Effect on reader is evaluated using relevant evidence.

Explanatory phrase used to show evaluation of effect on reader.

Effective use of detail from the source.

Critical and detailed evaluation that considers alternative ideas.

Detailed evaluation using a range of textual references.

Close focus on the question.

Explanatory phrase used to show evaluation of effect on reader.

Writer's methods are considered throughout the response, with embedded quotations used as part of explanatory sentences.

Writer's choice of language is considered and its effect evaluated.

Detailed evaluation of effects shows perceptive understanding of the writer's methods.

Shows perceptive understanding of narrative perspective.

Sophisticated terminology used to evaluate the effect of sentences.

Connotations of individual words are evaluated.

Explanatory phrase used to show evaluation and to keep a close focus on the question.

Ending of extract is evaluated

The sense of tension is broken slightly by the 'two men' who are 'chipping at the side of the ship', which does not sound threatening. However, there is still a sense of anticipation as the writer uses the adverb 'drowsy' to describe the 'stillness', suggesting nobody will hear or care if Dona gets into danger. Her thoughts are shared, making the narrative suddenly seem more intimate and allowing the reader to understand her fears. Her fears are articulated in a long sentence with repetition of the phrase 'no one', which reminds the reader that she is alone, and the choice of the word 'shrouded' is an effective way of increasing the sense of danger as it carries connotations of death.

The final man revealed on the ship is described with the simile 'like a monkey', which creates an exotic image for the reader, as it is an animal associated with distant lands. The sense of excitement is then increased as his singing starts 'softly' but gets 'a little louder', which suggests the danger is moving closer to Dona. It would also be clear to the reader that Dona is more excited than afraid as the verb 'straining' is used to show how closely she listens. The extract ends on an exciting cliffhanger as it is revealed the man is singing in French, which would have carried connotations of danger in the time of pirates.

A very strong answer because...

This is a strong answer that sticks closely to the focus of the question throughout. The student achieves this through phrases such as 'It is made to seem dangerous as', 'A sense of excitement is emphasised' and 'increasir the sense of danger'.

The student gives a clear overview at the start of their response, which sums up their critical judgement. They then go on to expand on this overview throughout the answer.

The evaluation is detailed and the adverbial 'However' highlights alternative ideas that the student explores. The student considers a wide range of methods used by the writer – such as the use of individual words and sentence types – and gives detailed explanations to evaluate the effects that these create.

A mixture of short, embedded quotations and concise paraphrasing support the points being made, and this makes the response very clear and easy to follow.

Other points could have been discussed, such as the fact that Dona is unseen by the men. However, it is not necessary to cover all possible points in order to evaluate the source fully.

SECTION B – Writing

You are advised to spend about 45 minutes on this section.

Write in full sentences. You are reminded of the need to plan your answer.

You should leave enough time to check your work at the end.

5 A magazine has asked for contributions for their creative writing page.
Either: Write a description of a journey as suggested by this picture:

Or: Write a story about finding something frightening.

(24 marks for content and organisation
16 marks for technical accuracy)
(40 marks)

Hint

Read the notes below. Then look at the sample answer to the Question 5 descriptive option on pages 74–75, and the sample answer to the Question 5 narrative option on pages 76–77.

Writing a good answer

Good answers will:

Content

- shape the reader's response by using tone, style and register effectively and convincingly
- match the tone, style and register clearly to purpose, form and audience
- use a wide range of ambitious vocabulary and use language features effectively.

Organisation

- be highly structured and well developed and link paragraphs smoothly
- include a range of convincing and complex ideas

Accuracy

- use a full range of sentence types correctly and for effect, and punctuate them accurately throughout
- use a wide range of punctuation and grammatical structures accurately
- use Standard English consistently and appropriately and use complex grammatical structures confidently
- have very few spelling mistakes, including ambitious vocabulary.

If answering the descriptive question, good answers are also likely to:

- focus clearly on description and avoid using too many narrative elements
- use an effective structure across the piece, such as a shift in focus between the general and the specific
- use a range of descriptive techniques, including careful use of figurative language

If answering the narrative question, good answers are also likely to:

- use a narrative structure, with clear parts that reflect what the question asks for (for example, if the question only asks for an opening, then the answer shouldn't include the end of the narrative)
- begin and end in an engaging and satisfying way.

Hint

Look at this sample answer to the Question 5 descriptive option. Refer back to the notes on page 73, then look to see how some of the points are used here.

Q5: sample answer

On the night we arrived, the horizon was dominated by a beautiful full moon, casting soft, silvery shadows onto the sun-bleached timbers of the deck. Behind it, millions of stars paled into pinpricks, sinking into the deep, dark blue sky, creating a dramatic backdrop to my first view of the ship. The sun, long since disappeared in a blaze of red and gold, had hung around only long enough to illuminate my fellow travellers, faces bleached with fear.

Silence fell over us as the starboard side of the ship loomed towards us, the only sound the light plop and slap of the oars on the water. The sea was calm; as black and impenetrable as ink but somehow friendly, lapping at the sides of the dinghy in small, welcoming waves. Suddenly, the Golden Hind towered above us like a vision from a child's picture book; a perfect realisation of the pirate ship from Peter Pan, complete with furled sails, rigging and a crow's nest swaying slightly in the warm night breeze.

The hand that reached down to pull us aboard did not disappoint. Leathery and calloused from years at sea, it belonged to a wizened man with a gravelly voice and a grey, straggly beard. Yet there the likeness to a fairy-tale pirate ended. There was no smile on his lips, no twinkle in his eye and no offer of a nip of rum to welcome us aboard. He made it clear we were here to work, and that the work would start that very night.

An endless round of deck scrubbing, galley clearing and sail mending filled nearly every waking minute from that point on. Having arrived pale and pasty, we soon became lean as we learnt to climb the rigging; hanging off ropes like monkeys and jumping down to negotiate slippery decks, we developed the rolling gait of life-long sailors. Eating and sleeping in shifts, the ship quickly became our life.

Annotations:

- Alliteration used to create an atmospheric image.
- Engaging opening that is clearly focused on the picture in the question.
- Verbs and adjectives used to create a vivid image.
- Personification and verbs used to develop image.
- Ambitious synonym for 'light up' or 'show'.
- Variety of sentence openings used to create interest.
- Adjectives and a simile used to create a vivid image.
- Interesting verb and engaging simile.
- Ambitious vocabulary choice.
- Alliteration of verb and adverb give rhythm to the writing.
- Build-up of adjectives creates a vivid image.
- Paragraph contains a variety of sentence types, with a short sentence in the middle, to emphasise contrasting ideas.
- Repetition used to create an idea of character.
- The idea of hard work used as an effective link between paragraphs
- Pattern of three used to highlight hard work.
- Ambitious sentence structure uses advanced punctuation correctly.
- Shorter sentence to emphasise the point.
- Draws on an idea in the fiction extract in Section A of the paper without plagiarising the source.

Dashes add additional information to create dramatic atmosphere.

Advanced punctuation used correctly, with ambitious and appropriate vocabulary.

Storms came and went; the only difference between them was our growing confidence in our skills. Our first – the edge of a tropical monsoon off the coast of Indonesia – sent grey clouds scudding across the sky while waves crashed into the side of the ship, lifting up and stealing anything we hadn't had time to tie down. Grey faces, tinged with green, fought to save the sails. Our second – a full-on tornado from the Gulf of Mexico – found us all up on deck in the teeth of the storm, steering confidently through the walls of water while lighting forked above us.

As days melted into weeks, and weeks became months, the wizened man became less reserved. His gravelly voice started to soften and his eyes, at first dark pebbles in the moonlight, started to crinkle at the edges as the hint of a smile began to smooth his features. We knew we had finally earned his respect when, tornado safely navigated, we were finally given our first taste of the ship's rum.

Now, standing steady in the crow's nest, I find myself gazing greedily at a tiny hint of land on the horizon. Directly ahead is a familiar town and a harbour: tiny wooden houses, donkeys pulling carts, small boats unloading the fish of the day. I lean forward into the breeze, breathing deeply as the scent of the land wafts across the boat. A solid, comforting, earthy smell of pine and peat with hints of animal; the smell of home. I've loved my four months at sea; but I'm ready to put my feet back down onto solid ground.

Personification and interesting verbs create powerful images.

Powerful imagery.

Ambitious verb used to suggest the passage of time.

Repetition of a previous image develops ideas.

Temporal (time) adverb used to structure the piece.

Change in tense suggests to the reader that the action has returned to the present day.

A positive image built up using a colon and a list.

A satisfying ending that concludes the overall idea of the piece, yet is still descriptive.

A very strong answer because...

This is a skilfully crafted and convincing descriptive piece, structured to take the reader from the general (the scene as a whole) to the particular (the ship and the character). The question asks for a description of a journey and the student skilfully keeps the focus on **description** rather than moving into narrative. Powerful descriptive techniques are used throughout to paint a vivid picture for the reader.

The student uses a variety of figurative devices with ambitious vocabulary to create strong images in the reader's mind – and these techniques do not break up the flow of the writing.

A range of structural features is used in an inventive way and to good effect. The sentence structure is varied throughout with some effective paragraph linking, while adverbial phrases are used to link the ideas and show the passage of time.

The ending is strong and carefully planned to create a satisfying resolution for the reader.

Set A
Paper 1 Answers

Hint

Look at this sample answer to the Question 5 narrative option. Refer back to the notes on page 73, then look to see how some of the points are used here.

Variety of sentence structures and openings.

Engaging opening uses repetition in a pattern of three.

Personification used to set the scene.

This is it. This is the moment. This is when I finally prove to myself that I can do it. In front of me swim row upon row of piercing eyes, all sparkling with eager anticipation. My heart pounds and my palms sweat as I inhale deeply and pull back my shoulders. Silence slowly creeps through the huge hall and the air becomes very still. Gripping the microphone tightly, I clear my throat and open my mouth to speak. Nothing happens. I freeze in fear.

I first froze on stage when I was only ten years old. A very shy, but extremely tall child, with bright red hair that resisted all of my mother's attempts to smooth it flat, I always felt most at home at the back of the class, as far away from the action as I could possibly get. Unsurprisingly, my size meant I was passed over for the speaking parts in the annual nativity play; in Year 5 I was to be behind Michael, another shy and clumsy boy, as the hind legs of the donkey.

We were both literally shaking with nerves when the big day dawned. Michael was physically sick. I was hyperventilating. No amount of reassurance from our lovely teacher Miss Spice could alleviate our trepidation. We were – despite having no lines and nothing to do except come on to the stage and stand still – completely terrified.

That walk out of the wings felt like a trek across burning coals. Swelteringly hot inside the thick, fluffy donkey suit, I gripped so tightly onto Michael that he cried out in pain and tripped over a shepherd's foot. Disaster struck as the donkey split into two and my head and torso burst out into the light. A century of silence was broken by stifled laughter that started at the back of the hall and swelled steadily until loud guffaws washed over me on to the stage. I burst into tears of shame.

I have never been able to muster the courage to put myself forward for any type of performance since that day. At school I was bullied before the play (being a foot taller than your classmates and having red hair makes you an easy target) but afterwards the chant of 'donkey' seemed to follow me down every hall and into every classroom. I spent so much time hiding from my tormentors in the toilets that I only narrowly missed failing all my GCSEs. Even now, answering a question in public sends an arctic chill down my back and makes my words come out all twisted and warped.

Short sentences used to create suspense and shape reader response.

Clear paragraph linking, and ambitious and controlled use of a change in tense for the flashback.

Well-structured multi-clause sentences create interesting rhythm.

Variety of sentence openings used for effect.

Effective and correct use of semi-colon.

Drama created through effective use of short sentences, with repetition of 'was'.

Ambitious vocabulary choices.

Effective use of advanced punctuation to create humour.

Figurative language– simile, and then metaphor – used to sum up narrator's feelings.

Alliteration used to create rhythm.

Effective paragraph link.

Ambitious use of advanced punctuation to create ironic tone.

Figurative language – metaphor – used effectively to reinforce feelings.

Interesting vocabulary choices.

Direct address to reader draws them in to end of story.

Pattern of three, with repetition of 'how', mirrors opening.

So, I hear you ask, why am I on a stage in front of you now? My mother is the reason. Whenever I came home so downhearted that I felt the world had ended, she was always there with a comforting hug and an uplifting word. She told me that no matter how brutal, how harsh or how cruel the taunts got, I would one day shake off my nerves and emerge from my protective shell. And, like all mothers, she was right.

The moment is here. This is it. My heart is still pounding and my hands are still clammy with sweat, but as I search for my mother's eyes amongst the sea of faces, I know I can finally do it. I take a breath, look straight ahead, and launch into the opening sentence of my speech.

Figurative language – metaphor – combines with ambitious vocabulary to hint at a positive ending.

Sophisticated control of structure as it repeats ideas and phrases from the opening paragraph, using short sentences for dramatic effect.

Clear and satisfying conclusion.

A very strong answer because...

This is a successful narrative because it shapes the reader's response, using suspense at the beginning and then going back in time to develop the narrator's character. The change in tense from present to past and then back again at the end is also skilfully handled – the tenses are maintained correctly throughout.

The student is careful not to use figurative language too frequently, which makes the examples of simile and metaphor that are included particularly powerful. Impressive vocabulary choices – for example, 'alleviate' and 'trepidation' – are used accurately for effect.

The student links paragraphs effectively, and uses an ambitious range of sentence structures for effect throughout the answer. The overall structure is particularly successful because the ending mirrors the opening with the use of repetition, short sentences and a pattern of three. This suggests the student has taken a few minutes to plan their answer before starting to write.

The pace of the ending is cleverly controlled. The student uses short sentences to echo the narrator's sense of confidence. The final sentence is carefully structured to end with a calm tone, as well as suggesting a sense of anticipation and achievement.

Hint

Turn to pages 17–18 to re-read the sources.

SECTION A – Reading
Answer ALL questions in this section.
You are advised to spend about 45 minutes on this section.

1 Read again the first part of **Source A** from **lines 1 to 13**.
Choose **four** statements below which are TRUE.

- Shade the **circles** in the boxes of the ones that you think are true.
- Choose a maximum of four statements.
- If you make an error cross out the **whole box**.
- If you change your mind and require a statement that has been crossed out then draw a circle around the box.

(4 marks)

A David Shariatmadari gives a large amount to charity every Christmas. ○

B £300 is a large part of David Shariatmadari's monthly budget. ●

C David Shariatmadari thinks £278 is a very generous donation to charity. ○

D David Shariatmadari gives money to two charities every month. ●

E At school, David Shariatmadari had no problems abseiling down a wall for charity. ○

F Raising money for charity by doing something physical doesn't come naturally to David Shariatmadari. ●

G David Shariatmadari feels uncomfortable giving away his money. ●

H David Shariatmadari has no concerns about the motives behind his charitable giving. ○

Only four statements are selected, which suggests the student has read the question carefully.

All statements selected are true, which suggests the student has read the lines in the source and the statements carefully before marking their answers.

Student has indicated their choices clearly by shading the circles in the relevant boxes.

2 You need to refer to **Source A** and **Source B** for this question.
Both sources discuss different things to consider when giving to charity.
Use details from **both** sources to write a summary of the differences between the things they mention.

(8 marks)

Hint

Read the notes below, then look at the sample answer on page 80.

Writing a good answer

Good answers will include:

- perceptive synthesis and interpretation of both texts
- perceptive inferences from both texts
- carefully chosen references or textual detail that is relevant to the focus of the question
- clear, relevant statements that show perceptive differences between the texts.

Possible points of difference between Source A and Source B:

- Source A discusses making regular contributions as well as a one-off 'generous donation', whereas Source B advises givers to 'set aside a proportion' of their income.
- Source A suggests 'big-time philanthropy' would be more than £278, whereas Source B suggests that people should donate 'a tenth of their income'.
- Source A mentions taking part in exciting events like abseiling to raise money, whereas Source B talks about 'Bazaars and sales', while 'stationery and stamps' hints at sending letters asking for contributions.
- Source B suggests that giving to charity should be focused on the people receiving the donation, however in Source A the act of giving is a 'selfish' one.

Student makes it clear which sources they are referring to throughout.

Opening sentence makes the point of the paragraph clear.

Hint

Look at this sample answer to Question 2. Refer back to the notes on page 79, then look to see how some of the points are used here.

Clearly structured paragraph, using an appropriate adverbial to introduce the point of difference.

Short embedded quotations used to present evidence from both sources.

Clear inferences made about both sources.

Each paragraph of the answer covers both sources equally.

Q2: sample answer

Both texts mention the amounts of money that could be donated to charity. The writer of Source A suggests that one way is to donate a 'small amount... each month', while another is to make a 'generous donation', which should be more than £278 to count as 'big-time philanthropy'. However, Source B says givers should 'set aside a proportion' of their income, ideally 'a tenth', suggesting that if everyone did this 'vast sums' would be raised.

The writer of Source A mentions taking part in exciting events, such as a sponsored abseil, as a way of raising money. However, the writer goes on to explain that he 'neglected to find any sponsors', which suggests that this may not be the most effective fund-raising method. In contrast, Source B puts forward the idea of 'Bazaars and sales', while the reference to 'stationery and stamps' implies sending out letters asking for contributions to good causes, although these methods involve 'huge expenditure'.

In Source B, there is 'no duty more plainly inculcated in the Bible' than giving to the 'deserving poor', and this should not be 'grudging or of necessity'. This suggests that it is important to think more about those who will receive the charity than oneself. However, in Source A 'those in need' are barely mentioned and a selfish attitude is seen as the best way to 'keep on giving'.

A very strong answer because...

This is a strong synthesis in which three relevant points are made and fully supported by relevant evidence. One of the strengths of this answer is that the student writes in well-structured paragraphs, covering both sources equally. The points are clear and supported with short, embedded quotations that are directly relevant. The student also makes successful inferences about both sources. In addition, adverbials such as 'however' and 'in contrast' make the differences between the sources clear.

Other points of difference between the sources could have been made, but this question is only worth 8 marks and it's not necessary (or possible, in the time available) to cover every difference in order to write a strong answer.

3 You now need to refer **only** to **Source B** from **lines 1 to 14**.
How does the writer use language to suggest giving to charity is difficult?

(12 marks)

Hint

Read the notes below, then look at the sample answer on page 82.

Writing a good answer

Good answers will include:

- **analysis** of the effects of the language chosen by the writer
- a carefully chosen range of textual details
- sophisticated and accurate use of subject terminology.

Possible language points:

- The piece starts with an anecdote/personal evidence to create a truthful tone.
- Formal vocabulary is used to set a serious tone – 'inculcated'.
- The use of 'but' in the opening sentence introduces a sense of argument.
- Alliterative adjectives are used to emphasise the negative side of giving to charity – 'immense', 'injudicious', 'ill-considered'.
- Noun phrases are used to create an emotive picture – 'poor crossing-sweeper boy', 'miserable woman begging'.
- The repetition of 'miserable' helps to build an emotive image.
- The pronoun 'we' is used to include the reader.
- A short sentence is used to create a lecturing tone in the middle of the second paragraph.
- The use of 'misplaced' marks the change in tone to lecturing.
- The prefix 'ill' is repeated for emphasis.
- Brackets are used for '(not her own)', creating a knowledgeable/warning tone.
- An expert opinion is used to emphasise and back up the warning given in the opening paragraphs – 'An experienced worker... stated...'.

Hint

Look at this sample answer to Question 3. Refer back to the notes on page 81, then look to see how some of the points are used here.

Focus on the question using accurate subject terminology.

Tone identified using relevant textual detail.

Clear link to question focus.

Sophisticated subject terminology used to support a point.

Effect of sentence types is considered.

Language device is identified and the effect explained.

Sophisticated use of subject terminology.

Relevant textual detail included as short, embedded quotations.

Analysis of the combined effect of vocabulary choice and language device.

A change in tone is identified and explained using accurate subject terminology and relevant textual detail.

Analysis of the overall effect of several sentence and language choices.

Effect of sentence length is considered.

Accurate use of subject terminology to comment on writer's point of view.

Sophisticated use of subject terminology.

Q3: sample answer

The source opens with a personal anecdote from a 'friend' about giving to charity, which sets a truthful tone. A slightly judgemental tone is created by the noun phrase 'deserving poor', which suggests disapproval and that giving to charity is not without problems.

The judgemental tone is then emphasised by a short sentence that uses three alliterative adjectives – 'immense', 'injudicious' and 'ill-considered' – to highlight the harm that can be done by some charitable giving. Emotive noun phrases such as 'poor crossing-sweeper boy' and 'miserable woman begging' are then used to build up an emotive picture that suggests the writer understands why people give to charity.

The writing then takes on the tone of a lecture, with a short sentence using the bold statistic 'nine cases out of ten' and ending with the harsh adjective 'misplaced'. In contrast to the emotive examples in the first part of the second paragraph, a multi-clause sentence is used to continue the story of the crossing-sweeper boy and the begging woman. The use of earlier examples makes the stories seem real and truthful, with the repetition of the prefix 'ill' creating a vivid image of the problems created by 'misplaced' charitable donations.

An expert opinion from an 'experienced worker in London' is then used to back up the writer's view that giving to charity can be a problem.

The final sentence goes back to consider those who do give on 'impulse'. The final clause is intended to scare readers about the dangers of giving to charity as the writer uses hyperbole to suggest that such giving causes 'great evils'.

Sophisticated use of subject terminology.

A very strong answer because...

This is an analytical answer that covers a wide range of examples in a concise and clear style. The writer's views are clearly identified and explained using relevant textual detail.

Accurate subject terminology is used with some sophisticated examples, such as 'noun phrase' and 'hyperbole'. The student also considers the overall effect of several language features, making some perceptive points abou their effect on the reader.

Other examples of language features and techniques could also have been used. However, it's not necessary (or possible, in the time available) to cover every possible language point in order to write a strong answer.

4 For this question, you need to refer to the **whole of Source A**, together with the **whole of Source B**.

Compare how the writers convey their different attitudes to giving to charity.

In your answer, you could:

- compare their different attitudes
- compare the methods they use to convey their attitudes
- support your response with references to both texts.

(16 marks)

Hint

Read the notes below, then look at the sample answer on pages 84–85.

Writing a good answer

Good answers will include:

- a **comparison** of ideas and perspectives in a perceptive way
- analysis of how writers' methods are used
- a carefully chosen range of supporting detail from both texts
- detailed understanding of the different ideas and perspectives in both texts.

Possible comparison points:

- The writer of Source A feels giving to charity is the right thing to do; the writer of Source B feels it can be harmful.
- Source A gives a personal story; Source B is more general.
- Source A focuses on the effects of giving on the writer; Source B focuses on how to give.
- Source A imagines the recipients of charitable giving in a general sense – 'a group of people whose lives are falling apart'; Source B gives details about the 'deserving poor'.
- Source A is personal opinion; Source B is practical advice.

Possible points about the writers' methods:

- Both sources use references that would be familiar to the original readers – Facebook and Twitter ('RT') in Source A; the Bible and traditional values in Source B.
- Source A uses a colloquial, informal style – 'belt-tightening', 'lives... falling apart'; the language of Source B is very formal –'inculcated', 'injudicious'.
- Source A is more conversational – 'As it happened...'; Source B uses emotive imagery – 'cruelly ill-fed'.
- Source A is a personal account, therefore the pronoun 'I' is used throughout; Source B aims to instruct the reader – 'we should', 'we must not forget'.
- Both writers include expert opinions.
- Source A includes facts – 'research reported in today's Times'; Source B offers mainly personal opinion – emotive language such as 'poor crossing-sweeper boy', 'miserable baby crying'.

Hint

Look at this sample answer to Question 4. Refer back to the notes on page 83, then look to see how some of the points are used here.

Clear opening statement that identifies differences in the writers' perspectives and focuses on the question.

Tone and purpose considered.

Short, embedded quotations used as supporting detail.

Close focus on the question.

Adverbial used to make comparison clear.

Difference in purpose considered.

Clear structure starting with similarity, commenting on Source A and then exploring difference in Source B.

Analysis of writer's methods.

Clear focus on question.

Adverbial used to make comparison clear.

Surname of writer used to refer to Source A.

Variety of language devices considered to support points.

Adverbials used to make comparison clear.

Continued focus on question.

Q4: sample answer

Overall, while they are both about giving to charity, the perspective of Source A is that giving to charity is positive regardless of the amount given, whereas the attitude of the writer of Source B is that some charity can be harmful.

The texts are very different in tone and purpose. Shariatmadari uses a conversational tone throughout to entertain, using colloquial terms such as 'belt-tightening' and 'falling apart'. His tone seems casual when he says he can afford to give on a 'whim' and his statement that his 'charitable habits are modest' suggests that he feels giving to charity is the right thing to do. In contrast, the writer of Source B intends to instruct readers, so a formal tone is used throughout, with complex vocabulary like 'inculcated' and 'injudicious' and precise instructions for 'successful almsgiving'.

Both texts consider why people give to charity. Shariatmadari does not find it easy. He admits to feeling 'uncomfortable' about giving to charity and anticipates the reader's disbelief at this statement by using direct address with the colloquial phrase 'I hear you say'. Shariatmadari appears to be confused about his reasons for giving, using the article to work through his feelings and coming to the conclusion that for most people, giving is 'selfish', although he still thinks it should be done. Source B on the other hand, takes a slightly judgemental tone, suggesting that people find giving easy, and seeming to find them rather foolish, calling them 'dear creatures' and stating that they give without using 'their judgement'.

Shariatmadari focuses throughout on the reasons why people give to charity, and the effect on the giver. He uses facts from the Times to measure his £300 gift against the average British donation and then uses expert opinion to write about the 'warm glow' that can come from donating. While he uses technical language to make the expert opinion seem trustworthy, he then sums this up by reverting back to colloquial language, ending with the short sentence 'Charity can get you high.' While Source B also uses expert opinion, here it is from an unnamed 'experienced worker', and, in contrast to Source A, is used to back up the writer's attitude to charity, which is that 'deserving' people are hard to find.

The tone of Source B then changes and the writer starts to instruct the reader, giving practical advice about how and when to give. The verb 'should' and the imperative 'set aside' are repeated several times to tell the reader exactly how and when to give. This would probably irritate modern readers, but it is typical of advice texts from the Victorian era. While the writer uses the inclusive 'we', the tone remains impersonal, and the writer is made to sound superior to the reader through the use of the formal pronoun 'one'. In contrast, Shariatmadari uses the pronoun 'I' throughout to tell a personal story, describing his experience of donating online, and he outlines his feelings in detail when another donation is taken from his bank account. His acknowledgement that he was so 'horrified' he 'gulped' and felt tricked sounds like a confession, and readers would probably respect his honesty. This would make his opinions about giving to charity seem very trustworthy.

Both texts use contemporary references to connect with their readers. Source A includes references to Facebook and Twitter, and uses the abbreviation 'RT', which assumes the audience is familiar with modern social media platforms. Source B, on the other hand, is rooted in very traditional Christian values; it uses words like 'blessing' and 'sanctified', and mentions the clergy. This style would probably have made Victorian readers take the advice seriously.

Variety of language devices considered to support points.

Analysis of effect of writer's methods on reader.

Perceptive comment about use of pronouns.

Perceptive comment that considers reader response.

Analysis of effect of writer's methods on reader.

Difference in reader appeal is considered.

A very strong answer because...

This answer shows a detailed understanding of the differences between the two sources. The student makes a range of comparisons, covering ideas, perspectives and different reader responses. All points include details from both sources and are supported with relevant evidence. The student considers and analyses the writers' methods, and considers a wide variety of language devices. Several perceptive points of comparison are made – for example, the point about the way both texts use personal pronouns and how in Source B this sounds superior, and the point about a reader's likely response to the confessional tone of Source A.

The student uses a clear paragraph structure, which makes the comparisons easy to follow. Both texts are given equal weighting throughout and the student stays focused on the question.

Other points could also have been included – for example, Source B uses emotive language to describe the recipients of charity in detail whereas Source A just imagines them. However, it's not necessary (or possible, in the time available) to include every possible comparative point, or to include every possible example of language used in order to write a strong answer.

Hint

Read the notes below. Then look at the sample answer on pages 87–88.

SECTION B – Writing

You are advised to spend about 45 minutes on this section.

You are reminded of the need to plan your answer.
You should write in full sentences.
You should leave enough time to check your work at the end.

5 'Taking part in events to raise funds for charity is a waste of time. It doesn't actually help anybody in the end.'

Write an article for a broadsheet newspaper in which you explain your point of view on this statement.

(24 marks for content and organisation
16 marks for technical accuracy)

(40 marks)

Writing a good answer

Content

Good answers to Question 5 will:

- match the tone, style and register clearly to the purpose, form and audience
- use a wide range of ambitious vocabulary
- shape language features and devices effectively throughout.

Organisation

Good answers to Question 5 will:

- be highly structured and well developed
- use a wide range of inventive structural features
- include a range of convincing and complex ideas
- link paragraphs smoothly.

Accuracy

Good answers to Question 5 will:

- use a full range of sentence types correctly and for effect, and punctuate them accurately throughout
- use a wide range of punctuation accurately
- use Standard English consistently and appropriately
- show strong control of complex grammatical structures
- have very few spelling mistakes, including ambitious vocabulary.

Good answers to this question are also likely to:

- include details about the benefits of giving to charity
- include examples of ways to give to charity
- use a variety of persuasive techniques such as facts, opinions and expert evidence
- include counter-arguments
- start and end with engaging ideas that fully support the viewpoint taken.

Personification used to create a strong image.

Engaging opening uses a short sentence to create reader interest.

Interesting verb.

Q5: sample answer

Yesterday I ran my first marathon. As I jostled my way to the start line my stomach did a somersault and my heart hammered in my chest. All those weeks and months of training seemed futile; I was never going to keep up with the lycra-clad athletes standing alongside me. They all looked supremely fit and quietly confident; I looked pasty-faced and extremely scared. When I eventually passed the finish line I tried very hard to ignore my screaming lungs, my aching calves and my blistered feet. After all, I was running to raise money for charity, so I should feel good, shouldn't I?

Happily, my ambivalence about giving to charity was as short-lived as my post-marathon exhaustion. But it seems that concern about charitable donations is on the rise. A recent report by *Which* magazine states that we are exposed to over 10 requests for our money every single day. Eighty per cent of those polled reported feeling overwhelmed with requests for money and told tales of being bombarded with requests for money in the street, over the internet and even on their own doorstep.

The report went on to say that many people now feel switched off from charity as they wonder how much of their donation actually gets to the cause they are supposed to be supporting. After all, those smiling young people who turn up on your doorsteps wielding pictures of emaciated dogs or cute cats are paid to part you from your hard-earned money. And they probably get a bonus for signing up more than their quota.

However, please remember that without our direct debits many smaller charities would struggle to survive. For every multi-million-pound organisation like Oxfam – which employs thousands of aid workers across the world and spends 25 per cent of its income on administration – there is a local charity operating on a shoe string to help vulnerable people in your area. For instance, in my town, a van is used to deliver groceries, library books and medicine to housebound elderly people. The people who run it take no salary, but rely on fundraising events and donations to pay the van's running costs. For the recipients of their service, the visits are a lifeline.

Hint

Look at this sample answer to Question 5. Refer back to the notes on page 86, then look to see how some of the points are used here.

Interesting verb and alliteration used to help draw the reader in.

Ambitious vocabulary choice and advanced punctuation.

Contrast used in a carefully structured sentence.

Rhetorical question and personal pronoun used to manipulate reader response.

Adverb used at start of a sentence with ambitious vocabulary.

Expert opinion, facts and statistics used to support a point.

List of three used to emphasise a point.

Clear link between paragraphs.

Focus on statement in the question, which anticipates reader response.

Ambitious vocabulary choices.

Adverbial used to signpost counter-argument.

Advanced punctuation used to add emphasis.

Colloquial term used to make tone more personal and emotive.

Direct appeal to reader.

Personal anecdote used and developed to back up a point.

Development of viewpoint with further idea.

Ambitious vocabulary and metaphor used to describe atmosphere.

Variety of sentence types and lengths add pace and rhythm to the writing.

Small amount of colloquial language used to create an informal, friendly tone.

Ambitious vocabulary choices.

Giving to charity also carries a very real benefit for those who donate. The marathon I ran was organised to raise money for a second van, one capable of taking people to and from vital hospital appointments. Hundreds of townspeople turned out to run or act as marshals, and the atmosphere was electric; everywhere I looked there was a sea of smiling faces cheering me on. People who rarely see their neighbours came out to mingle and chat on the High Street, a Facebook page was created to share pictures of the day and a barbeque was held in the local park to celebrate those who ran. A really positive community spirit was created. To be honest, we all had such a blast that the money we raised just seemed like an added bonus.

So my advice to charity sceptics is to think local. Find a cause you really believe in that makes a big difference in a small place and offer to get involved. You don't have to give loads of money, you could help as a volunteer – that way you could address your fears and find out exactly how the donations are being spent.

You could even put on your trainers and follow my lead by entering a marathon. Even with blistered feet I still felt pretty good about the money I had raised. And I'm certainly a whole lot fitter.

Final short paragraph links back to opening.

Imperatives used to signal advice.

A very strong answer because...

This is a well-planned and carefully controlled piece of writing. It starts off with an engaging personal descriptio that would encourage a reader to think about their own views. From the start, the student uses interesting and appropriate language features in a controlled variety of sentence types. Figurative language is not used too frequently, which makes the examples that are included highly effective. The student also occasionally uses carefully chosen colloquial language, which helps to stop the tone from becoming too formal.

Facts and statistics are used to introduce expert evidence, which shows that the student is considering the viewpoint in the question statement. One of the main strengths of this article is that the writer's viewpoint focuses on just one personal and very specific idea about local charities. This is developed with interesting and appropriate detail into a persuasive argument.

Spelling is accurate throughout. The student also makes occasional and accurate use of advanced punctuation – such as semi-colons and dashes – to create an effective variety of sentence types and lengths.

SECTION A – Reading
Answer ALL questions in this section.
You are advised to spend about 45 minutes on this section.

Read again the first part of the source from lines **1** to **2**.
List **four** things from this part of the source about the Aspen sisters' journey.

(4 marks)

1 It was after the death of their brother

2 'at the end of February'

3 In a Daimler

4 'through a sudden fall of snow'

Hint

Turn to page 33 to re-read the source.

Question 1 is only worth 4 marks, so the student lists four short, relevant points.

The student answers with short paraphrases or quotations – it's fine not to write in full sentences for this question.

Alternative answers

Answers to Question 1 could also include:

- they were returning to Evensford
- they came by car.

Hint

Read the notes below, then look at the sample answer on page 91.

2 Look in detail at this extract from **lines 7 to 14** of the source:

> It was so cold that solid ice seemed to be whipped up from the valley on the wind, to explode into whirlwinds of harsh and bitter dust that pranced about in stinging clouds. Ice formed everywhere in dry black pools, polished in sheltered places, ruckled with dark waves at street corners or on sloping gutters where wind had flurried the last falls of rain.
>
> Frost had begun in the third week of January, and from that date until the beginning of April it did not leave us for a day. All the time the same dark wind came with it, blowing bitterly and savagely over long flat meadows of frozen floods. There was no snow with it until the afternoon the Aspen sisters came back; and then it began to fall lightly, in sudden flusters, no more than vapour, and then gritty and larger, like grains of rice.

How does the writer use language here to describe the weather?

You could include the writer's choice of:

- words and phrases
- language features and techniques
- sentence forms.

(8 marks)

Writing a good answer

Good answers will include:

- analysis of the effects of the **language** chosen by the writer
- carefully selected (short) quotations or close reference to the text to back up the points being made
- sophisticated and accurate use of subject terminology.

Possible language points:

- Action verbs emphasise the harsh effects of the weather – 'whipped', 'explode'.
- The verb 'explode' makes the ice seem sudden and dangerous.
- The adjectives 'harsh' and 'bitter' sound unpleasant/aggressive.
- The use of personification – 'pranced' – suggests exaggerated dancing.
- The metaphor 'dust' creates an image of something that gets everywhere.
- The increasing use of words with connotations of precision and danger helps to build up a sense of the harsh weather – 'stinging', 'polished', 'dark waves'.
- A sinister image is created with 'dark waves' followed by 'street corners'.
- The phrase 'dark wind' sounds bleak/sad.
- Adverbs emphasise the harsh weather – 'bitterly', 'savagely'.
- The use of 'meadows' creates contrast and exaggerates the effect of the frost.
- The final multi-clause sentence is split into two by a semi-colon, emphasising the change brought by the Aspe sisters.
- The final sentence links the sisters to the falling snow, suggesting they will bring change that may be 'gritty' c uncomfortable.
- The simile 'like grains of rice' suggests something that will spread and get into everything.

Opening sentence is clearly focused on the question and identifies overall tone of the extract.

Accurate subject terminology is used to comment on sentence type and its effect.

Correct subject terminology is used to identify technique, with clear explanation of effect.

Hint

Look at this sample answer to Question 2. Refer back to the notes on page 90, then look to see how some of the points are used here.

Q2: sample answer

A picture of harsh weather is built up by the very first multi-clause sentence. The action verbs 'whipped' and 'explode' suggest the ice has come suddenly and is dangerous, and the adjectives 'harsh' and 'bitter' build on this by highlighting the aggressive nature of the cold weather. The metaphor 'dust' to describe the ice creates an image of something that gets into everything and cannot be escaped. This is further emphasised through personification using the verb 'pranced', which suggests the ice is dancing about in an exaggerated manner. The writer then creates a slightly sinister image using the verb 'stinging' followed by the adjective 'polished', which has connotations of something painful but precise and sharp.

The second paragraph continues this image of harsh and dangerous weather with the adverbs 'bitterly' and 'savagely' juxtaposed with the word 'meadows', drawing the reader's attention to the damaging effects of the frost. The final sentence is split into two with a semi-colon, which creates a sense of drama about the Aspen sisters' return. They are associated with the coming of the snow, which is perhaps a metaphor for the effect they will have on the town. The simile 'like grains of rice' suggests that the sisters, like the weather, will spread and get into everything.

Short, embedded quotations used throughout the answer.

A second language feature is identified – shows an understanding that different techniques are combined to build up and emphasise particular effects.

Imagery – metaphor – is identified and its effect explained.

Language device – personification – explained using accurate subject terminology.

Two language techniques identified to support an advanced explanation of the effect of the imagery.

Sophisticated use of subject terminology to explain complex points.

The effect of punctuation is explained.

Language device – simile – explained using accurate subject terminology.

Close focus on question is maintained throughout.

A very strong answer because...

This answer analyses a wide range of language features and techniques in a style that is clear and to the point. The student stays focused on the question throughout, and the opening sentence shows a clear understanding of the way the weather is presented in the extract.

Subject terminology is used accurately – in particular, the student uses the term 'juxtaposed' in a sophisticated way to explain a complex point about the writer's use of imagery. Quotations are short and relevant, and the student embeds them effectively into clear explanatory sentences.

Other examples of language features and techniques could also have been used. For example, the student could have mentioned the sinister image created by the 'dark waves'. However, this question is only worth 8 marks and it's not necessary (or possible, in the time available) to cover every possible language point in order to write a strong answer.

Hint

Read the notes below, then look at the sample answer on page 93.

3 You now need to think about the **whole** of the source.
This text is taken from the opening of a novel.
How has the writer structured the text to interest you as a reader?
You could write about:
- what the writer focuses your attention on at the beginning
- how and why the writer changes this focus as the source develops
- any other structural features that interest you.

(8 marks)

Writing a good answer

Good answers will include:

- analysis of the effects of the **structural** features chosen by the writer
- carefully selected (short) quotations or close reference to the text to back up the points being made
- sophisticated and accurate use of subject terminology.

Possible structural points:

- The source is structured to emphasise the separation between the bitter cold outside and the women inside the car.
- The source is sequenced so that it opens with the Aspen sisters but then withholds information about them, which creates suspense.
- The focus shifts to the weather, and detailed descriptions create a slow pace, building suspense.
- Descriptions of the weather build up a harsh picture, foreshadowing Lydia's arrival.
- Repeated ideas about the bad weather mean that Lydia's arrival is associated with bitter, harsh conditions.
- The perspective starts in the valley, then moves gradually towards the town, and then to the narrator's view from the window.
- The focus shifts to the car and the way it skids, then narrows again.
- The topic changes to snow, which starts to fall at the same time as the sisters arrive, perhaps foreshadowing the effect Lydia has on the narrator.
- The white snow is contrasted with the black clothes of the Aspen sisters.
- The Aspen sisters are described first, then Lydia is finally revealed.
- The narrator is inside the building looking out, emphasising his fascination with Lydia.
- The focus ends on Lydia Aspen, with a description that starts with her hair, then narrows in on her eyes.
- The final, short one-sentence paragraph creates a cliffhanger for the reader.

Clear opening sentence gives an overview of the effect of the structure.

Explanation of the effect of the opening, using sophisticated subject terminology.

Short, embedded quotations used to back up points made.

Q3: sample answer

Overall, the structure of the extract creates a contrast between the outside world, with detailed descriptions of the harsh weather, and the inside of the car. The extract opens by withholding information, which creates suspense about the arrival of Lydia Aspen – the reader is only told that the sisters arrive in a 'Daimler' with 'gilt monograms'. The focus then immediately shifts out to the weather and zooms slowly back in, with detailed descriptions used to create a slow pace. This in turn creates a sense of suspense for the reader as it emphasises the importance of Lydia's arrival.

There is a close focus on the weather which moves from the general to the particular, starting in the valleys and then taking the reader on a slow journey into the town. Here, the narrator lingers to describe the High Street before narrowing the focus further onto 'dark waves' on 'street corners' and 'sloping gutters'. This creates a harsh picture, and is perhaps intended to foreshadow the effect Lydia's arrival will have.

The text then narrows down further to share the narrator's perspective, first of the car, then of the occupants who are slowly revealed in turn, with the actual arrival of Lydia Aspen delayed until the very end of the final sentence. This narrowing of perspective highlights the fact that the narrator is inside looking out, which makes Lydia seem even more mysterious. Her importance to the narrator is then emphasised in a new paragraph, starting with her hair and finally narrowing in to her eyes, emphasising the narrator's fascination with the girl. A final one-sentence paragraph is then used to create tension about the effect Lydia will have on the narrator's life.

Subject terminology used to highlight a key structural point.

Explanatory phrase used to show understanding of the effects of structural choices.

Effect on reader considered.

Use of accurate subject terminology.

Shows understanding of the way the description is structured.

Sophisticated use of terminology shows perceptive understanding.

Explanation extended to show detailed understanding, using sophisticated terminology.

Shows understanding of the shift in focus from setting to characters.

Identifies the effect of narrative perspective.

Shows perceptive understanding of the effect of the ending.

Understanding of the effect of the short final paragraph.

A very strong answer because...

This answer considers a wide range of structural features including changes in focus, the withholding of information and the pace of the extract. Accurate subject terminology is used throughout, and the student includes short, embedded quotations where necessary to support the points being made.

Alternative answers might have emphasised the link between Lydia's arrival and the repeated ideas about the harsh weather, or commented on the contrast created between the white of the snow and the black clothes of the sisters.

Hint

Read the notes below, then look at the sample answer on pages 95–96.

4 Focus this part of your answer on the second part of the source **from line 15 to the end**.

A student, having read this section of the text, said: 'The writer builds a real sense of drama before introducing Lydia Aspen. This makes you really appreciate why the narrator finds her so fascinating.'

To what extent do you agree?

In your response, you could:
- write about your own impressions of Lydia Aspen's arrival
- evaluate how the writer has created these impressions
- support your opinions with references to the text.

(20 marks)

Writing a good answer

Good answers will include:
- detailed and critical **evaluation** of the effect on the reader
- a perceptive understanding of the writer's methods and their effects
- carefully selected and relevant textual detail as evidence for all points being made
- a clear and close focus on the question.

Possible evaluative points:
- A link is made between the snow beginning to fall and the arrival of the Aspen sisters.
- The writer uses the description of the weather to create tension/drama.
- Lydia's arrival is closely associated with bitter, harsh weather.
- The juxtaposition of the contrasting phrases 'darkened whirl of wind' and 'flowered into whiteness' suggests the arrival of the sisters will be dramatic.
- The narrator almost seems trapped watching the scene – 'nursing the wrist' suggests he is a bystander waiting for something to happen.
- The narrator's view is obscured by the windows 'partly glazed over' with 'a pattern of starry fern'.
- The car drives past steps that are like 'a waterfall of chipped glass', linking the sisters' arrival with something broken and dangerous.
- The skidding of the car creates a dramatic picture for the reader, suggesting danger.
- Lydia is revealed slowly and with an air of mystery, unlike her aunts, who are described in a more straightforward manner.
- Lydia's name is not used in the final paragraph that describes her, adding to the sense of mystery.
- The description of Lydia's 'long coils of black hair', and her hood, creates a dangerous image.
- In the final line, the reader can identify with the narrator's sense of fascination.

Short, embedded quotations are used to support points in a convincing way.

Overview given at the start of the answer addresses the first part of the statement in the question.

Hint

Look at this sample answer to Question 4. Refer back to the notes on page 94 to see how some of the points are used here.

Q4: sample answer

The writer builds a strong sense of drama by linking the falling of the snow with the arrival of the Daimler carrying the Aspen sisters, and by delaying the mention of Lydia for as long as possible. A sense of tension is created as the snow is described in detail, with the adjective 'frozen' and the simile 'like a waterfall of chipped glass' suggesting something dangerous. This sense of danger surrounding the arrival of the sisters is effectively emphasised by the juxtaposition of two contrasting ideas – the 'darkened whirl of wind' that 'flowered into whiteness' – which might make the reader feel that something new and exciting is about to happen.

A sense of drama and tension is also created as the narrator is presented as trapped by the window, 'nursing' a sprained wrist, and the narrative becomes more of a personal recollection with the use of the pronoun 'I'. This encourages the reader to empathise with the narrator's perspective, although there is a sense that his recollections may not be entirely accurate as the reader may remember that the view from the window is 'partly glazed over' with 'starry fern'.

The writer uses a sequence of harsh verbs separated by the repetition of 'and' to build the drama even further with a description of the car skidding and then righting itself. The Aspen sisters are then revealed to the narrator separately through the skidding movement, again encouraging the reader to see their arrival as dramatic and tense. The sisters are presented as very contrasting individuals: the first appears from a 'confusion of leopard rugs', which carries connotations of an exotic wild animal, and the second 'bounced like a rosy dumpling', suggesting someone round and friendly. A tense atmosphere is created around the younger sister through the writer's choice of verbs — 'shudder', 'snatching', jolted' and 'clutching' – which all create a vision of somebody sharp and a little frightening. The narrator's first memory of Lydia is her appearance from behind this sister, which suggests to the reader that he remembers her arrival as something dramatic, exciting and perhaps life-changing.

Writer's methods are considered and their effect clearly evaluated.

Use of explanatory phrase shows evaluation of effect on reader.

Perceptive understanding of the writer's methods.

Use of 'also' shows evaluation is being developed and the student is keeping a close focus on the question.

Evaluation of the change in narrative perspective shows perceptive understanding of the writer's methods.

A critical and convincing point, as the student evaluates the change in narrative perspective by considering something from earlier in the extract.

The writer's methods are considered throughout the response, with embedded quotations used as part of explanatory sentences.

The structure of the extract is evaluated, with a close focus on the question.

Inference is used to comment on relevant textual details.

Atmosphere and tone are considered, with comments on the writer's methods used to support the point.

The reader can then understand the narrator's fascination with Lydia as the writer dedicates an entire paragraph to describing her, but without using her name. The use of 'she' creates a sense of mystery and danger. This is continued when the first thing the reader finds out about her is that she has 'long coils of black hair'. While the narrator only sees 'part of her face' for a 'moment', the writer makes his fascination for her clear by drawing out this first glance with a multi-clause sentence. The choppy effect of the sentence encourages the reader to share the narrator's fascination, as it suggests the hesitation and uncertainty of infatuation which the reader might relate to from their own youth.

Clearly addresses the second part of the statement in the question.

The phrase 'This is continued' shows this is a detailed evaluation.

Effect of sentence types is evaluated and the effect on the reader is clearly considered.

Ends with a critical judgement about reader response that clearly addresses the focus of the question.

A very strong answer because...

This strong answer starts with a clear overview, using a phrase from the question to establish a clear focus. The student then takes a chronological approach to the evaluation, following the order in the text; this keeps the focus on the sense of drama in the source.

Reader response is carefully considered. For example, the student gives a detailed explanation of the way the reader is encouraged to empathise with the narrator's perspective, as well as with his fascination with Lydia.

The student considers the effects of a wide range of methods used by the writer, including both language features (such as sentence types) and structural techniques (such as the juxtaposition of ideas).

A mixture of short, embedded quotations and concise paraphrasing support the points being made, and this makes the response very clear and easy to follow.

Remember that it is not necessary to cover all possible points in order to evaluate the source fully.

SECTION B – Writing

You are advised to spend about 45 minutes on this section.

Write in full sentences. You are reminded of the need to plan your answer.

You should leave enough time to check your work at the end.

5 You are going to enter a creative writing competition.
Your entry will be judged by a panel of people of your own age.
Either: Write a description suggested by this picture:

Or: Write the opening part of a story about meeting somebody for the first time.

(24 marks for content and organisation
16 marks for technical accuracy)

(40 marks)

Hint

Read the notes below. Then look at the sample answer to the Question 5 descriptive option on pages 98–99, and the sample answer to the Question 5 narrative option on pages 100–101.

Writing a good answer

Good answers will:

Content

- shape the reader's response by using tone, style and register effectively and convincingly
- match the tone, style and register clearly to purpose, form and audience
- use a wide range of ambitious vocabulary and use language features effectively.

Organisation

- be highly structured and well developed and link paragraphs smoothly
- include a range of convincing and complex ideas

Accuracy

- use a full range of sentence types correctly and for effect, and punctuate them accurately throughout
- use a wide range of punctuation and grammatical structures accurately
- use Standard English consistently and appropriately and use complex grammatical structures confidently
- have very few spelling mistakes, including ambitious vocabulary.

If answering the descriptive question, good answers are also likely to:

- focus clearly on description and avoid using too many narrative elements
- use an effective structure across the piece, such as a shift in focus between the general and the specific
- use a range of descriptive techniques, including careful use of figurative language

If answering the narrative question, good answers are also likely to:

- use a narrative structure, with clear parts that reflect what the question asks for (for example, if the question only asks for an opening, then the answer shouldn't include the end of the narrative)
- begin and end in an engaging and satisfying way.

Hint

Look at this sample answer to the Question 5 descriptive option. Refer back to the notes on page 97, then look to see how some of the points are used here.

Engaging opening that creates intrigue for the reader.

Alliteration in the choice of adjectives, which is extended in the choice of verbs and nouns throughout the paragraph.

Effective personification of the ice vapours helps draw the reader in to the cold of the scene.

Q5: sample answer

That morning I was woken up by the chill of the ice. Its vapours, crisp and cutting, slid under the bedroom door and crept through the frosted glass of the window, curling their way across the carpet until they reached my nostrils, pink with cold. The duvet, which on most nights was almost too hot, had joined forces with the ice and locked it in around me. The only way to escape was to get up and move.

I sat, peering through the frozen pane. The ice storm – which we had waited for with trepidation – had arrived in the night: its power, even in the first light of dawn, was obvious. In the garden below a robin hopped forlornly around the flowerbeds, hoping to surprise a worm. My eyes followed him and together we discovered that the bird table had been toppled and now lay across the lawn: a fallen soldier.

The grass, like everything else, was coated in white – not a delicate, icing-sugar white but a treacherous, crunchy white that stuck up in sharp peaks. A few blades struggled through the unwelcome blanket in search of the sun, but the sky was filled with thick cloud which made a weird glow, leaving the world shivering below. The robin flew to a branch of the old apple tree and I lifted my eyes.

The drive was like a ribbon, its surface smooth and glazed. Standing steady now in the calm of the morning, the shrubs that bordered the lawn had been battered by the biting winds but had survived. A sudden sound startled the robin, who moved on to the wrought iron gates at the end of the drive, and I heard the engine of our neighbour's car as he backed it, straining against the cold, onto the road.

I sat on, peering through the frozen pane. The steaming mug of tea in my hands at last began to warm my numb fingers and I stretched them out. Looking up again, I found the icy scene had disappeared – the windows all fogged up from my breath and the warmth of the tea. I cleared a patch of the fog with my sleeve and looked for the robin.

Advanced sentence structure – with ambitious vocabulary – uses sophisticated punctuation to emphasise the power of the storm.

Ambitious choice of adverb adds character and detail.

Strong choice of synonym for 'find'.

Effective paragraph link – the idea of the lawn is picked up at the start of the new paragraph with 'the grass'.

Powerful metaphor emphasises the strength of the storm.

Ambitious noun phrase creates a vivid image.

Effective choice of verb and noun phrase.

Focus shifts effectively throughout the piece from the immediate surroundings (the bedroom, the garden) to the larger scene (the road) and back again (the garden, the sister).

Simile used to add atmospheric detail.

Ambitious verbs and adjective, with alliteration to add pace.

The senses are used to add depth to the description.

Repetition from earlier paragraph is used to emphasise the narrator's position as an observer.

Repeated references to the cold weather throughout the piece for emphasis.

Effective paragraph link.

Interesti[ng] vocabula[ry] choices.

Advanced punctuation – semi-colon – to introduce a new focus (the road).

Effective variety of sentence lengths and structures, with a dash before 'but not today' to emphasise the unusual conditions.

He was still on the old iron gates and beyond them I could see the road; the tree-lined avenue swept just past the house before turning away from us towards the town. On each side of the road, the trees threw out long, naked branches, their thin white limbs reaching out towards one another. Slush decorated the kerbs and the tarmac gleamed with water. It was nearly rush hour and the road was usually gridlocked at this time on a weekday – but not today.

The neighbour's car had long since gone and all was quiet. Waiting. A flock of birds swooped low and then up onto the roof of the bus shelter and then I saw the power lines slumped across the road. Lifting my eyes further I could see that, beyond the cables, a tree was down and, beyond that, the flashing lights of emergency vehicles. There would be no school today and I was happy. Like the world outside, I was waiting …

A flicker in the garden below caught my eye and the robin was there again, this time with a worm in his beak. Above him the clouds were slowly starting to break, letting through a few thin rays of sun. Then he was gone, up and over the gates, across the road and out of sight.

And then I saw her. A small figure in the distance, all wrapped up and wobbling slowly along the slippery pavement, one arm stretched out for balance, the other dragging a heavy suitcase. As she got closer, I could see her breath curling in the icy air. My sister was home from university at last.

Weakness of the trees provides an effective contrast to the power of the storm described throughout the piece.

Ambitious vocabulary choices.

Effective range of sentence openers used throughout.

Minor sentence used to create tension.

Interesting choice of verbs.

Repetition of 'beyond' highlights the wider scene, contrasting it with the narrator's position inside.

Effective link between the scene outside and the narrator inside.

Repetition of 'waiting' helps to build tension.

Advanced punctuation – ellipsis – adds to tension.

Ambitious choice of noun.

Repetition of 'then' adds pace.

Effective choice of synonym for 'moving'.

Strong ending, with detail that reminds the reader of the 'vapours… curling' in the opening paragraph.

A very strong answer because...

This is an effective descriptive piece that is skilfully structured to take the reader from the narrator's immediate surroundings (the bedroom) to the wider scene (the road) and then back again to close detail (the sister). The student successfully keeps the focus on description rather than allowing narrative to take over.

The student uses a variety of figurative devices, with ambitious vocabulary to create powerful images in the reader's mind. The techniques that are used include examples of carefully chosen metaphor, simile, personification, repetition, reference to the senses, and strong choices of individual words, including some effective synonyms. These techniques do not break up the flow of the writing.

A range of structural features is used effectively. The student uses a variety of sentence openers to help the description flow, and different sentence lengths and types are used thoughtfully to control the pace of the piece. The minor sentence 'Waiting.' is particularly strong and introduces a sense that something is about to happen. Accurate punctuation is also used successfully to create pace and tension.

The ending is skilfully structured to slowly reveal to the reader the reason for the narrator's wait at the window.

Hint

Look at this sample answer to the Question 5 narrative option. Refer back to the notes on page 97, then look to see how some of the points are used here.

Engaging opening that is clearly focused on the task.

Suspense created as reader is not told who the girl is.

Ambitious vocabulary choice.

Convincing colloquial phrases used to show character and to suit audience.

Q5: sample answer

I crashed the car the first time I saw her in the flesh. So mesmerised was I by the sight of her that I only narrowly missed hitting her at the lights. Slamming on the brakes to the accompaniment of squealing rubber, the car careered up the pavement straight into a lamppost. The crunch and scrape of concrete on metal filled the car as my head bounced off the exploding air bag, sending tiny stars to dance around in front of my eyes. 'Typical', was my first thought, 'I finally get the chance to meet her and blow it by nearly mowing her down.'

I had first heard of her years before, during the long, hot summer of '14 when Jed joined our gang. Standing six feet tall, with the type of blonde hair that's more usually seen on surfing adverts, he set all the girls' hearts beating just a little bit faster; while us boys just wanted to be him. I can still remember where we were when he first showed us his sister's photo: in the park, whiling away another interminably long, hot summer afternoon.

Most people remember that summer because of the heat. It landed in late June and stayed with us right through until early September. There seemed nowhere to escape it: it leaked into houses and lay, like a greasy film, on every surface. Just walking outside meant razors of hot air prickled at your skin and the smell of hot tarmac pinched your nostrils. But I barely registered the weather. For me that summer was all about a girl I hadn't even met.

At first, I thought he was showing us a picture of a famous model or actress. She was simply stunning. All the usual clichés applied: she had long blonde hair, sun-kissed skin, and a smile that lit up her face. I had heard about love at first sight (my younger sister went on about relationships incessantly) but, like most teenage boys, I was way too cool for that type of mushy romance stuff. So I put on a nonchalant act and barely glanced as he scrolled through a series of family photos.

Variety of sentence openings.

Adjectives and verbs used to create strong imagery.

Inventive structure, taking reader back in time to provide background and draw out moment of meeting in order to create suspense.

Ambitious sentence structure uses commas to embed a clause and then a semi-colon to add a contrasting point.

Advanced punctuation, with colon used between two clauses to add an explanation.

Ambitious verb followed by interesting adverb.

Sophisticated personification of the weather.

Ambitious description, with figurative language (simile).

Metaphor and the senses used to help the reader feel the heat.

Short sentences used to create a contrast and emphasise the narrator's feelings; also brings focus back to task.

Brackets used to add an 'aside' that is appropriate for a younger audience.

Ambitious vocabulary used to show character.

Colloquial language used to show character of narrator.

Variety of sentence structures, including a list.

Effective paragraph link.

We always stayed until the last of the light stretched out over the park, but I left early that day. The setting sun reached out into distant flowerbeds and sent giant shadows chasing across the scorched earth. But I noticed nothing. I was desperate to get home and search Jed on social media. I spent that night flicking through his pictures and greedily drinking in every possible sighting of his gorgeous sister. She appeared to live a life straight out of a magazine; all designer labels, expensive yachts and weekends in the country. Despair set in as I realised there was absolutely no way she would be interested in a 17-year old schoolboy from a boring market town who still lived with his mum and dad.

I tried to put her out of my mind. Learning to drive provided a welcome distraction. Years of computer gaming meant I had razor-sharp reflexes and I was soon executing perfect three-point turns and hill starts. A small inheritance from a distant relative meant I could afford an intensive course of lessons and still have enough left over to buy a small hatchback. Sailing through my test first time, I was soon the most popular member of the gang and spent the end of the summer holidays ferrying my friends around town.

Ironically, I had just dropped Jed off at the gym when I saw her. I knew straight away it was her; my online stalking had become an obsession and I looked at her face so often I knew it better than my own. For a very short moment everything went still and very silent, and then I looked up and our eyes met. She said nothing, just stared back at me without even blinking.

Personification used to create a vivid image.

Sentence variety used to create tension.

Ambitious verbs and adverb.

Ideas are appropriate for audience.

Variety of sentence structures to maintain pace and interest.

Ambitious vocabulary choices.

Some more formal language and structure balances colloquial phrasing elsewhere, showing sophisticated crafting of piece.

Narrative returns to starting point.

Tension is built up with a long multi-clause sentence and repetition of 'and', before the final cliffhanger.

A very strong answer because...

This is an effective narrative that successfully draws on ideas in the fiction extract in Section A of the paper with its use of structure and descriptions of the weather – and the student achieves this without plagiarising the source.

The writing is compelling and incorporates ideas, such as first love, that are appropriate to a teenage audience. The structure is uncluttered but also imaginative: key information is withheld to create tension and build towards a cliffhanger that is completely suitable as the opening of a longer story. The student juggles a complex timeline effectively, using a flashback technique that adds to the impact of the narrative. The student also uses an extensive range of figurative and language devices with confidence, which builds the description without swamping the colloquial tone of the narrative. Sentences are varied and the student uses a wide range of punctuation to great effect. Spelling and grammar are both accurate and clear.

Hint

Turn to pages 49–50 to re-read the sources.

Only four statements are selected, which suggests the student has read the question carefully.

All statements selected are true, which shows that the student has read the lines in the source and the statements carefully before marking their answers.

SECTION A – Reading
Answer ALL questions in this section.
You are advised to spend about 45 minutes on this section.

1 Read again the first part of **Source A** from **lines 1 to 13**.
Choose **four** statements below which are TRUE.

- Shade the **circles** in the boxes of the ones that you think are true.
- Choose a maximum of four statements.
- If you make an error cross out the **whole box**.
- If you change your mind and require a statement that has been crossed out then draw a circle around the box.

(4 marks)

A Peter Cummins is the first male nanny to graduate from a London college. ○
B Peter Cummins played rugby when he was at school. ●
C Peter Cummins travelled the world on a gap year. ○
D Peter Cummins enjoyed working as a male au pair. ●
E Nannies may need to work long hours. ●
F Peter Cummins was the only student from Wales at Norland. ○
G Before training as a nanny, Peter Cummins took career advice. ●
H Only 2% of the students at Norland are male. ○

Student has indicated their choices clearly by shading the circles in the relevant boxes.

2 You need to refer to **Source A** and **Source B** for this question.

Both sources are about nannies.

Use details from **both** sources to write a summary of the differences between Peter Cummins and the nannies described in Source B.

(8 marks)

Hint

Read the notes below, then look at the sample answer on page 104.

Writing a good answer

Good answers will include:

- perceptive synthesis and interpretation of both texts
- perceptive inferences from both texts
- carefully chosen references or textual detail that is relevant to the focus of the question
- clear, relevant statements that show perceptive differences between the texts.

Possible points of difference between Source A and Source B:

- Peter Cummins cleans up the kitchen and 'is careful to load the dishwasher'; whereas Source B says that the nannies are not expected to do housework, 'scrub floors' or 'carry coals'.
- Peter Cummins does craft activities and plays 'energetic games' with the children he looks after, suggesting that his training includes the role of playmate; whereas the training of the 'nurses' in Source B is more focused on the children's physical health, including how to prepare 'poultices'.
- Peter Cummins does not have to wear a uniform as 'there is no male equivalent'; however, the 'cornflower blue beige' uniform of the nannies in Source B is described in some detail.
- Peter Cummins is 'a former schoolboy rugby prop', suggesting he is physically strong; however, the nanny described in Source B is 'delicate-looking'.

Hint

Look at this sample answer to Question 2. Refer back to the notes on page 103, then look to see how some of the points are used here.

Opening sentence makes the point of the paragraph very clear.

Both sources are covered equally throughout the answer.

Q2: sample answer

Both texts mention the type of work nannies have to do. The writer of Source A says that Peter Cummins cleans the floor, which suggests that he sees housework as an important part of the job. However, Source B suggests that household chores are not part of a nanny's role as the 'nurse' is not expected to 'scrub floors' or 'carry coals'.

According to one employer, Peter Cummins made 'paper airplanes' and did 'foot painting' with the children in his charge and played 'really energetic games with them'. This suggests that his role was partly to be a playmate and to encourage the children in craft and sporting activities. In contrast, the main focus of the nannies at Norland in the 19th century appears to have been the physical health of the children, as they were given lessons in how to prepare 'poultices' and are referred to in Source B as 'nurses'.

Source B devotes two paragraphs to the uniform worn by the trainees at Norland, which is described as 'pretty'. The writer goes on to explain that the length of the dress was 'anxiously debated'. This suggests that it was important for nannies to look very feminine yet formal, and not to appear too provocative. In contrast, the writer of Source A explains that wearing a uniform is now a 'rare event' for modern nannies, which suggests that the role of a nanny is now more personal and informal.

Short, embedded quotations are used as textual detail to support points.

Relevant inferences made about both texts.

Each paragraph covers a new point of difference and covers both sources.

Each point of difference is supported by inferences about both sources, as well as quotations from each text.

Adverbial used to highlight the difference.

A very strong answer because...

This is a well-structured answer that covers both sources equally and draws relevant inferences from each. All points are supported by evidence, which the student presents effectively as short, embedded quotation The student also uses adverbials such as 'however' and 'in contrast' to make the differences between the sources clear.

Other points of difference between the sources could have been included, but this question is only worth 8 marks and it's not necessary (or possible, in the time available) to cover every difference in order to write a strong answer.

3 You now need to refer **only** to **Source A** from **lines 16 to 29**.
How does the writer use language to show that Peter is an unusual nanny?

(12 marks)

Hint

Read the notes below, then look at the sample answer on page 106.

Writing a good answer

Good answers will include:

- **analysis** of the effects of the language chosen by the writer
- a carefully chosen range of textual details
- sophisticated and accurate use of subject terminology.

Possible language points:

- The phrase 'female-dominated' suggests that men will find it hard to get work as nannies, or that men do not want to do the work.
- The colloquial phrase 'really got his hands dirty' suggests that Peter's approach to his role as a nanny was surprising.
- The long list of different activities – such as 'foot painting and playing football' – shows how Peter 'spent his days' and there are no negative comments, which suggests that his hard work and energy are unusual.
- Government statistics are included to show that targets for attracting more men into childcare are low, which emphasises that even the government thinks it is unusual for men to want to work in this profession.
- An expert opinion from The Daycare Trust is included, which admits that it is difficult to recruit men and it is 'a very long-term aim'.
- The slogan 'He Who Cares Wins' is an example of word-play and links to the SAS motto 'Who Dares Wins', suggesting that men need extra persuasion to become nannies.
- The repetition of 'female-dominated' in the first paragraph and then 'Female domination' in the last paragraph highlights how unusual Peter is as a nanny because he is male.
- The short sentence with the vague description of the male toilets as 'down in the basement somewhere' shows that even Norland College is not well-prepared for male students.
- We are told 'there is no male equivalent' for the famous Norland uniform, which reinforces the idea that Peter is an unusual nanny as he 'had to wear a suit' at the end of term.

Q3: sample answer

The writer shows that Peter is an unusual nanny by including a quotation from him that highlights the fact that he is different from most nannies because he is a man – Peter says he was warned that childcare was 'very female-dominated'. The word 'dominated' has connotations of control, which suggests that women are in charge and that it is unusual for men to work in this profession.

Clear focus on question from the start.

Language feature identified.

Individual word choice analysed using subject terminology.

Hint

Look at this sample answer to Question 3. Refer back to the notes on page 105, then look to see how some of the points are used here.

A quotation is then used from a parent who chose to have 'a male nanny' and was pleased with how Peter played 'really energetic games', which suggests that this is unusual for a nanny. The colloquial phrase 'really got his hands dirty' also implies that Peter's behaviour was unexpected. These examples reinforce the idea that Peter is not a typical nanny. The writer adds to this with a list of all the activities Peter did as a nanny. The list is long and includes a wide variety of activities such as 'foot painting and playing football' and we are told that this is how Peter 'spent his days'. This emphasises how hard Peter worked and the fact that nothing negative is said about him suggests that his energy and enthusiasm are unusual.

The writer then introduces a statistic. This focuses on how difficult it is to recruit male nannies as, while there is 'a target level of 6%', even this low figure 'looks quite ambitious'. An expert opinion is then used to back this point up, emphasising this is 'a very longterm aim'. This language highlights the difficulties in attracting men to the profession and this makes Peter seem even more unusual. Furthermore, The Daycare Trust uses the slogan 'He Who Cares Wins', which is a play on the SAS motto 'Who Dares Wins'. This shows that nannying is an unusual career for men and suggests they need to feel there is a masculine element to the job before they will consider it.

The last paragraph repeats the earlier reference to 'Female domination' for emphasis. This is followed by a short sentence which describes the male toilets vaguely as 'down in the basement', with the addition of 'somewhere' to create a humorous tone. This highlights how even Norland College is unprepared for male students. Finally, the reference to the Norland uniform, for which 'there is no male equivalent', further reinforces Peter's unusual status.

Detailed analysis of meaning.

Subject terminology used correctly and followed by an analysis of the effect.

Detailed analysis that identifies another language feature to develop a point.

Language feature identified using accurate subject terminology.

Short, accurate quotations embedded to support point.

Language feature identified.

Perceptive and detailed analysis of language features.

Language feature identified.

Analysis of the combined effect of sentence type and word choice.

Language choices and their effects across the whole extract are analysed.

A very strong answer because...

This is an analytical answer that covers a wide range of examples in a concise and clear style. One of its strengths is the way the student analyses the combined effect of several language choices.

Other examples could also have been included. However, it's not necessary (or possible, in the time available) to cover every possible language point in order to write a strong answer.

4 For this question, you need to refer to the **whole of Source A**, together with the **whole of Source B**.

Compare how the writers convey their different attitudes to childcare and being a nanny.

In your answer, you could:

- compare their different attitudes
- compare the methods they use to convey their attitudes
- support your response with references to both texts.

(16 marks)

Hint

Read the notes below, then look at the sample answer on pages 108–109.

Writing a good answer

Good answers will include:

- a **comparison** of ideas and perspectives in a perceptive way
- analysis of how writers' methods are used
- a carefully chosen range of supporting detail from both texts
- detailed understanding of the different ideas and perspectives in both texts.

Possible comparison points:

- Both sources are positive about Norland.
- Source A highlights a modern perspective about childcare; Source B emphasises Norland's 'rules', suggesting that the writer approves of a more formal, rigid structure.
- Both sources show that Norland nannies are well paid.
- Both writers mention the high costs of training at Norland.
- Source A presents nannying as a fuller role, which includes entertaining the children; Source B puts the emphasis on the nursing side of nannying.
- Source A is a very personal account about one nanny; Source B presents a more general picture of the Norland Institute.
- Both sources mention difficulties: Source A discusses the difficulties of being a male nanny; Source B mentions possible difficulties in the relationship between nannies and their employers.
- Both sources discuss something very new: Source A talks about Norland's first male nannies; Source B is about the new Norland Institute.
- Source A is about a well-educated graduate trainee, suggesting that thorough training is important; Source B says that Norland is for those who are unable to undertake a 'long course of professional training', implying that the writer feels nannying is a less demanding option than some other professions.

Possible points about the writers' methods:

- Source A uses a colloquial and informal tone – 'Marty Poppins', 'hadn't a clue'; the language of Source B is formal and serious – 'endowed', 'intellectual'.
- Both sources include expert opinions – Source A quotes parents and someone from Norland; Source B quotes Norland's Principal.
- Both writers end by expressing personal opinions – Source A mentions the high cost of training; Source B talks about how hard the 'road' ahead will be.
- Source A uses colloquial language and quotations from Cummins to entertain – 'I ended up looking after a family with six children'; Source B uses formal language and facts to inform – 'with an annual rise of £2'.

Hint

Look at this sample answer to Question 4. Refer back to the notes on page 107, then look to see how some of the points are used here.

Clear overview of perspectives with a focus on the question.

Both sources and their writers are clearly identified.

Clear inference with a focus on the question.

Analysis of writer's methods to consider tone.

Range of textual detail used to analyse writer's methods.

Adverbials used regularly to signpost comparison.

Clear comparison to previous point made about Source A.

Short, embedded quotations used in analysis of language.

Clear paragraph structure used to make comparison clear.

Detailed comparison using a range of ideas to support one comparative point.

Q4: sample answer

Both texts are about the training offered to nannies at Norland College but they offer different perspectives on childcare. In Source A, Roland White uses colloquial phrases such as 'got his hands dirty' to highlight that Norland nannies like Peter have a very modern perspective on childcare. However, in Source B, Rosa Nouchette Carey emphasises her more traditional attitude by focusing on Norland's 'rules for employer and employed', which suggests she agrees that childcare needs to be formal and structured.

Source A uses informal language to create a light-hearted, entertaining tone, starting with a play on words in the headline – 'Marty Poppins', a reference to the film 'Mary Poppins'. White includes a quote from Cummins to highlight how much he enjoys being a nanny and uses a list to outline duties such as 'foot painting and playing football', which emphasises the entertainment side of nannying and makes it sound like a modern and fun occupation. In contrast, Source B starts on a serious, factual note by quoting the prospectus, which uses formal, complex language such as 'endowed' and 'intellectual', stressing the serious nature of childcare. In contrast to Source A, Carey presents nannying as more of a nursing role, with training given in preparing 'poultices' and 'simple remedies'.

Both texts suggest that Norland College is offering something new in childcare, and that this is admirable. In Source B, Carey calls the probationers 'young crusaders' and presents the training as new and quite daring, describing it as a 'new untried' path of 'womanly independence'. There is an emphasis on the physical appearance of the probationers with the adjectives 'delicate-looking' and 'youthful' used in the description, which suggests that Carey sees childcare as only suitable for older, tougher women. Similarly, in Source A, White presents Cummins as an unlikely nanny, describing him as a 'former schoolboy rugby prop', which immediately draws attention to his masculinity, rather than to the caring attributes most usually associated with nannies. Like the probationers in Source B, Cummins is also presented as something of a fascinating pioneer – he was 'warned' against childcare as a profession but 'pressed ahead' as 'the only male' at Norland.

Similarity in language device identified, with difference in effect fully explained.

Clear identification of sources and their writers throughout.

Both texts mention the wearing of uniforms. In Source B, Carey again stresses the feminine nature of the probationers by describing the uniform as 'very pretty' and 'wonderfully becoming to bright complexions and fair hair', which suggests she feels that appearance is very important to a 19th-century nanny. This is also highlighted by the mention of the length of the dress, which was 'anxiously debated', and expert opinion from the Principal is used to back up this point. In Source A, White also uses a quotation from a Norland source about uniform, but he treats the matter in a more light-hearted way, using the adverb 'luckily' when explaining that uniforms are now rarely required.

Both texts end with a personal opinion. After detailing how many jobs Cummins has to choose from, White appears shocked at the cost of the training, using a colon after the short colloquial phrase 'He'll need the money' to emphasise how high the costs are. In contrast, in Source B, Carey uses the final paragraph to write about the 'difficulties' to come, and uses the idiom 'no road on earth is free from thorns' and the word 'trials' to suggest her view that childcare is a challenging occupation.

Full range of sentence and punctuation choices analysed.

Sophisticated terminology used to analyse writer's methods.

Focus on question from beginning to end of answer.

A very strong answer because...

This answer shows a detailed understanding of the differences between the two sources. The student makes a range of comparative points, all of which are fully supported by textual references. The writers' methods are considered and analysed, and the student explores a wide variety of language devices, including sentence types and punctuation.

The student uses a clear paragraph structure in this response. An introductory sentence outlines the comparative point, and a point is then made about each text in turn, fully supported by relevant evidence. Both texts are given equal weighting throughout and the student stays focused on the question.

Other points could also have been included – for example, the writers' attitudes to the educational background of the nannies they describe, or their perspectives on the nannies' pay and conditions. However, it's not necessary (or possible, in the time available) to include every possible comparative point, or to include every possible example of language used in order to write a strong answer.

Hint

Read the notes below. Then look at the sample answer on pages 111–112.

SECTION B – Writing

You are advised to spend about 45 minutes on this section.

You are reminded of the need to plan your answer.

You should write in full sentences.

You should leave enough time to check your work at the end.

5 'Schools are still pushing students into traditional gender roles. This is wrong – men are more than capable of childcare and women should be inspired to go into careers like engineering or science.'

Write the text of a speech for an event at your school or college in which you persuade young people of your own age to agree with your point of view on this statement.

(24 marks for content and organisation
16 marks for technical accuracy)
(40 marks)

Writing a good answer

Content

Good answers to Question 5 will:

- match the tone, style and register clearly to the purpose, form and audience
- use a wide range of ambitious vocabulary
- shape language features and devices effectively throughout.

Organisation

Good answers to Question 5 will:

- be highly structured and well developed
- use a wide range of inventive structural features
- include a range of convincing and complex ideas
- link paragraphs smoothly.

Accuracy

Good answers to Question 5 will:

- use a full range of sentence types correctly and for effect, and punctuate them accurately throughout
- use a wide range of punctuation accurately
- use Standard English consistently and appropriately
- show strong control of complex grammatical structures
- have very few spelling mistakes, including ambitious vocabulary.

Good answers to this question are also likely to:

- include examples of traditional male or female professions
- include examples of men or women in roles that don't traditionally match their gender
- use a variety of persuasive techniques such as facts, opinions and expert evidence
- include counter-arguments
- start and end with engaging ideas that fully support the viewpoint taken.

Everyday idiom creates an informal tone suitable for audience and purpose.

Engaging opening that suits audience and purpose.

Advanced punctuation used before engaging rhetorical question.

Hint

Look at this sample answer to Question 5. Refer back to the notes on page 110, then look to see how some of the points are used here.

Q5: sample answer

When I grow up I want to be a premier league football commentator. I live, sleep and breathe football – so what better way to earn a living than to spend all day talking about my passion? Sharing this with my form tutor recently, I was taken aback when my ambition was greeted not by enthusiasm but by an indulgent smile and a request to start being serious.

Crushed, I took my dream to the school's careers officer. His reaction was worse (I heard the word 'delusional'). He sent me away with a bunch of further education brochures, telling me to research 'something in catering'. It was then that the penny dropped. You see, I'm not your usual football commentator type. For one thing: I'm a girl.

If you're a girl who aspires to be the next Lewis Hamilton, or a boy who doesn't dare tell anybody he wants to be an infant teacher, then you'll share my pain. Despite two female Prime Ministers, too many schools are still pushing students into traditional gender roles. A recent study by a leading university found that only 12 percent of primary school teachers are men and only 3 percent work in nurseries. On the other hand, despite equal opportunities legislation, over 80 percent of barristers are male, and women account for only 7 percent of the UK firefighting force.

Notwithstanding the fact that this is completely unacceptable for young people living in the 21st century, schools are missing out on the chance to have a positive impact on the future of our society.

For instance, reversing traditional gender stereotypes around childcare can have definite advantages. Peter Cummins, the first male nanny to graduate from Norland College, faced huge opposition when he announced his intention to work in childcare. 'I was warned that I would face huge resistance from employers,' he said, 'but the reverse was true. All my employers found me to be a very positive role model for their young children, particularly the boys.' Many reports cite the lack of role models as the cause of many instances of anti-social behaviour, so surely more males in the caring professions is to be encouraged?

Variety of sentence lengths and openings creates appropriate pace for speech.

Ambitious vocabulary choices.

Synonym for 'ambition' used to avoid repetition and link effectively to 'aspires' in the next paragraph.

Sophisticated use of advanced punctuation to add humour.

Effective use of verb as sentence opening.

Variety of sentence structures and advanced punctuation used to create tension and manipulate audience response.

Clear paragraph link.

Clear focus on question.

Statistics and research used as evidence.

Colloquial vocabulary used to create an informal register.

One sentence paragraph to introduce new solution.

Section A reading source used as evidence, and care taken to avoid copying from the texts exactly.

Ambitious vocabulary choices.

Correct use of punctuation for a quotation.

Sophisticated conjunction used to link paragraphs.

Ambitious synonym for 'childcare'.

Development of point.

Repetition to link this paragraph with the previous one.

Sophisticated use of advanced punctuation.

Repetition in a pattern of three to emphasise point.

Pronoun 'we' used to include audience and call them to action.

Ambitious use of verb.

Pattern of three used to emphasise ideas.

Ends on personal, light-hearted note, which uses advanced punctuation and two contrasting sentence types.

Encouraging more girls to climb higher up the corporate ladder would also benefit wider society. Research suggests that companies run by women score higher in surveys about employee wellbeing and have a lower staff turnover. The same research cites a local fire station that hired a female firefighter: apparently, six months after her appointment, the employees reported less aggression, less stress and less harmful competitive rivalry.

And we certainly need to offer girls like me something more than the chance to perfect our skills in the kitchen. Female scientists should be invited into schools to inspire us into traditionally male subjects, female engineers should be hired to give talks at assemblies and work experience should be opened up to girls at local football clubs.

I'm certainly not going to allow outdated gender ideas to hold me back – I'm off for a week's placement at Trent FM radio and will push as hard as I can for a spot on the sports desk. Listen out for me next week!

A very strong answer because...

This is a well-planned and carefully controlled piece of writing that is perfectly suited to the audience and purpose. It starts off by engaging the audience with an interesting statement; this is followed by a personal anecdote that keeps a close focus on the statement in the question. The student uses a personal anecdote and idiom to create a light-hearted tone throughout the piece – this is highly appropriate for a speech aimed at a younger audience. Despite this relaxed tone, ambitious vocabulary choices such as 'delusional' and 'cite' stop the writing from becoming too informal.

The student uses facts and statistics to introduce research, creating a counter-argument to the viewpoint in the question statement. One of the Section A reading sources is also used effectively, and the student achieves this without copying anything from that text exactly.

One of the strengths of the writing is the careful way the student uses rhetorical devices to manipulate the audience's response; devices such as repetition are not used too often, which makes the examples that are included very effective. The conclusion is particularly successful as it returns to the ideas used at the start of the speech to end on an upbeat, positive note – again, an element that is very appropriate for the form (speech and the audience.

Spelling is accurate throughout, as is the punctuation for quotations. The student also makes occasional and accurate use of advanced punctuation – such as dashes and brackets – to create an effective variety of sentence types and lengths.

For your own notes

For your own notes

For your own notes

For your own notes

For your own notes

Published by Pearson Education Limited, 80 Strand, London, WC2R 0RL.

www.pearsonschoolsandfecolleges.co.uk

Copies of official specifications for all Pearson qualifications may be found on the website: qualifications.pearson.com

Typeset and illustrated by York Publishing Solutions Pvt. Ltd., India
Editorial and project management services by Haremi Ltd
Cover illustration by Miriam Sturdee

First published 2018

21 20 19 18
10 9 8 7 6 5 4 3 2 1

British Library Cataloguing in Publication Data
A catalogue record for this book is available from the British Library

ISBN 978 1 292 21325 5

Printed in Italy by L.E.G.O. S.p.A

Acknowledgements
The author and publisher would like to thank the following individuals and organisations for permission to reproduce copyright material.

1 Hachette UK: Frenchman's Creek by Daphne du Maurier, Sourcebooks, 9781402217104, pp43-44
3 Hachette UK: Frenchman's Creek by Daphne du Maurier, Sourcebooks, 9781402217104, pp43-44
17 Guardian News and Media Limited: Giving to charity is selfish – and that's fine by David Shariatmadari https://www.theguardian.com/commentisfree/2015/apr/07/giving-to-charity-is-selfish **18 Victorian Era:** From How to Give http://www.victorianvoices.net/ARTICLES/GOP/Charity/1897-Giving.pdf **33 Bloomsbury Publishing:** Love for Lydia by H. E. Bates, Methuen, 9780413776532, pp9-10 **35 Bloomsbury Publishing:** Love for Lydia by H. E. Bates, Methuen, 9780413776532, pp9-10 **49 Times Newspapers Limited:** Parenting: Marty Poppins is taking charge in the nursery https://www.thetimes.co.uk/article/parenting-marty-poppins-is-taking-charge-in-the-nursery-76bcsxvchlq
50 Religious Tract Society: The Girl's own paper, A new occupation for girls http://www.victorianvoices.net/ARTICLES/GOP/Work/1893-Nursing.pdf **66 Hachette UK:** Frenchman's Creek by Daphne du Maurier, Sourcebooks, 9781402217104, pp43-44 **90 Bloomsbury Publishing:** Love for Lydia by H. E. Bates, Methuen, 9780413776532, pp9-10

Photographs
Alamy Stock Photo: EXImages 43,97
Shutterstock: iurii 11,73

Notes from the publisher
Pearson has robust editorial processes, including answer and fact checks, to ensure the accuracy of the content in this publication, and every effort is made to ensure this publication is free of errors. We are, however, only human, and occasionally errors do occur. Pearson is not liable for any misunderstandings that arise as a result of errors in this publication, but it is our priority to ensure that the content is accurate. If you spot an error, please do contact us at resourcescorrections@pearson.com so we can make sure it is corrected.